PROJECT SUCCESS 4

Barry Bakin
Robyn Brinks Lockwood
Jenni Currie Santamaria

Series Consultants
Susan Gaer
Sarah Lynn

Pearson

Blake Schrock
Sales & Assessment Advisor
English Language Learning

Blake.Schrock@pearson.com
+1 570-220-0922
linkedin.com/in/blakeschrock

pearson.com/languages

PROJECT SUCCESS 4

Pearson Education, 10 Bank Street, White Plains, NY 10606

Staff Credits: The people who made up the *Project Success* team, representing editorial, production, design, and manufacturing, are Peter Benson, Andrea Bryant, Maretta Callahan, Iris Candelaria, Aerin Csigay, Mindy DePalma, Dave Dickey, Christine Edmonds, Nancy Flaggman, Ann France, Aliza Greenblatt, Gosia Jaros-White, Caroline Kasterine, Amy Kefauver, Niki Lee, Jaime Lieber, Jessica Miller-Smith, Tracey Munz Cataldo, Laurie Neaman, Jenn Raspiller, Julie Schmidt, Kim Snyder, Katherine Sullivan, Loretta Steeves, Jane Townsend, Ken Volcjak, and Martin Yu.

Interior Design: Word & Image

Cover Design: Ann France and Tracey Munz Cataldo

Text Composition: TSI Graphics

Text font: Franklin Gothic

For photo and illustration credits, please turn to the back of the book.

Library of Congress Cataloging-in-Publication Data

Lynn, Sarah.
 Project success : skills for the 21st century / Sarah Lynn ; Series Consultants: Susan Gaer, Sarah Lynn.
      pages cm
 Summary: Project Success is a blended-learning digital and print course with a strong focus on workplace skills, career readiness, and 21st century challenges. This unique video-based series engages learners with high-interest video vignettes that represent a "day in the life" of characters in diverse workplace settings that may simulate their own. Integrated skills lessons encourage critical thinking and problem solving woven into the students' English language learning journey.
 ISBN 978-0-13-294236-2 — ISBN 978-0-13-248297-4 — ISBN 978-0-13-294238-6 — ISBN 978-0-13-294240-9 — ISBN 978-0-13-294242-3 — ISBN 978-0-13-298513-0
 1. English language—Textbooks for foreign speakers. 2. English language—Spoken English. 3. English language—Sound recordings for foreign speakers. 4. English language—Study and teaching—Foreign speakers—Audio-visual aids. 5. Business communication—United States—Vocational guidance. I. Gaer, Susan. II. Title.
 PE1128.L98 2014
 428.2'4—dc23
                                                                              2013035851

ISBN-10: 0-13-294242-9
ISBN-13: 978-0-13-294242-3

Printed in the United States of America

15 2023

Contents

Acknowledgments

The authors and publisher would like to offer sincere thanks to our Series Consultants for lending their expertise and insights and for helping shape the course.

Susan Gaer Santa Ana College School of Continuing Education, Santa Ana, CA

Sarah Lynn Harvard Bridge to Learning and Literacy Program, Cambridge, MA

In addition, we would like to express gratitude to the following people. Their kind participation was invaluable to the creation of this program.

Consultants

Robert Breitbard, Director of Adult & Community Education, Collier County Public Schools, Naples, Florida; **Ingrid Greenberg**, Associate Professor, ESL, and Past-President, Academic Senate, Continuing Education, San Diego Community College District, San Diego, California; **Vittoria G. Maghsoudi-Abbate**, Assistant Director, Mt. Diablo Adult Education, Mt. Diablo USD, Concord, California; **Irina Patten**, Lone Star College-Fairbanks Center, Houston, Texas; **Maria Soto Caratini**, Eastfield College DCCCD, Mesquite, Texas; **Claire Valier**, Palm Beach County, Florida; **Jacqueline S. Walpole**, Director, Adult Education, Prince George's Community College, Largo, Maryland.

Reviewers

Eleanor Brockman-Forfang, Instructor, Special Projects (ESL), Tarrant County College, South Campus, Fort Worth, TX; **Natalya Dollar**, ESL Program Resource Coordinator, North Orange County Community College District, Anaheim, CA; **Bette Empol**, ESL, ABE, GED Prep and Bridge Coordinator, Conejo Valley Adult School, Thousand Oaks, CA; **Mark Fisher**, Lone Star College-Fairbanks Center, Houston, TX; **Ann Fontanella**, ESL Instructor, City College of San Francisco, San Francisco, CA; **Ingrid Greenberg**, Associate Professor, ESL, and Past-President, Academic Senate, Continuing Education, San Diego Community College District, San Diego, CA; **Janet Harclerode**, Santa Monica College, Santa Monica, CA; **Laura Jensen**, ESL Instructor, North Seattle Community College, Seattle, WA; **Tommie Martinez**, Fresno Adult School, Fresno, CA; **Suzanne L. Monti**, ESOL Instructional Specialist, Community College of Baltimore County, Continuing Education, Baltimore, MD; **Kelly Nusz**, Carlos Rosario Charter School, Washington, D.C; **Irina Patten**, Lone Star College-Fairbanks Center, Houston, TX; **Ariel Peckokas**, Collier County Public Schools Adult Education, Naples, FL; **Sydney Rice**, Imperial Valley College, Imperial, CA; **Richard Salvador**, McKinley Community Schools of Arts, Honolulu, Hawaii; **Maria Soto Caratini**, Eastfield College DCCCD, Mesquite, TX; **Patty Swartzbaugh**, Nashville Adult Literacy Council, Nashville, TN; **Candace Thompson-Lynch**, ESL Instructor, School of Continuing Education, North Orange County Community College District, Anaheim, CA; **Esther M. Tillet**, Miami Dade College-Wolfson Campus, Miami, FL; **Adriana Treadway**, Assistant Director, Spring International Language Center, University of Arkansas, Fayetteville, AR; **Monica C. Vazquez**, ESOL Adjunct Instructor, Brookhaven College, DCCCD, Farmers Branch, TX.

Thanks also to the teachers who contributed their valuable ideas for the Persistence Activities: **Dave Coleman**, Los Angeles Unified School District, Los Angeles, CA; **Renee Collins**, Elk Grove Adult and Community Education, Elk Grove, CA; **Elaine Klapman**, Venice Community Adult School, Venice, CA (retired); **Yvonne Wong Nishio**, Evans Community Adult School, Los Angeles, CA; **Daniel S. Pittaway**, North Orange County Community College District, Anaheim, CA; **Laurel Pollard**, Educational Consultant, Tucson, AZ; **Eden Quimzon**, Santiago Canyon College, Division of Continuing Education, Orange, CA.

Special thanks also to **Sharon Goldstein** for her skilled writing of the pronunciation strand.

SERIES CONSULTANTS

Susan Gaer has worked as an ESL teacher since 1980 and currently teaches at the Santa Ana College School of Continuing Education. She is an avid user of technology and trains teachers online for TESOL and the Outreach Technical Assistance Center (OTAN). Susan is a frequent presenter at local, state, national, and international conferences on using the latest technology with adult learners from the literacy level through transition to college. She has co-authored books and teacher's manuals, served on the executive boards for CATESOL (California Teachers of English to Speakers of Other Languages) and TESOL, and contributed to standing committees for professional development and technology. Susan holds a master's degree in English with emphasis in TESOL from San Francisco State University and a master's degree in Educational Technology from Pepperdine University.

Sarah Lynn has over twenty-five years of teaching experience in ESOL. She has dedicated much of her teaching life to working with low-level learners with interrupted education. Currently she teaches at the Harvard Bridge Program, Harvard University. As a teacher trainer, Sarah has led professional development workshops throughout the United States on topics such as teaching in the multilevel classroom, learner persistence, twenty-first-century skills, self-directed learning, collaborative learning, and scaffolding learning for the literacy learner. As a consultant, she has written ESOL curricula for programs in civics, literacy, phonics, and English language arts. As a materials writer, she has contributed to numerous Pearson ELT publications, including *Business Across Cultures, Future, Future U.S. Citizens*, and *Project Success*. Sarah holds a master's degree in TESOL from Teacher's College, Columbia University.

AUTHORS

Barry Bakin is in his twenty-sixth year of teaching ESL for the Division of Career and Adult Education (DACE) of the Los Angeles Unified School District. As an ESL Teacher Advisor for DACE, he trained instructors in instructional methods with a focus on promoting the introduction and integration of technology into the ESL curriculum. Barry has presented numerous workshops at local, regional, and international TESOL conferences on ways to use computer software and the Internet with ESL students. He is currently an online technology trainer for OTAN (The Outreach and Technology Assistance Network of the Sacramento County Office of Education) and is also a "Mentor of Mentors" in OTAN's Technology Integration Mentor Academy. Barry has a master's degree in instructional technology.

Robyn Brinks Lockwood has taught ESL in adult education, in intensive English programs, and at the university level. She currently teaches English for Foreign Students as part of the Language Center at Stanford University and serves as the coordinator for the American Language and Culture summer program. She has given numerous presentations at international, regional, state, and local conferences throughout the United States. Ms. Lockwood has authored and edited a variety of ESL textbooks, ancillary materials, and online courses. She holds a master's degree in English from Northwest Missouri State University.

Jenni Currie Santamaria has a masters degree in TEFL/TESL from San Francisco State University and has taught ESL and EL Civics for over twenty years. Her ESL experience includes middle school, adult school, community college, and university levels, and she has also taught EFL in Barcelona, Spain. She has served as a curriculum developer, technology mentor, and EL Civics coordinator. Her publications include a four-skill coursebook for adults and a children's dictionary, as well as numerous teacher's guides. She has been a contributing writer for reading, grammar, and speaking/listening series and has created many online/interactive activities. Currently, she teaches at ABC Adult School in Cerritos, California.

Scope and Sequence 4

Unit	Listening/Speaking VIDEO	Grammar VIDEO	Practical Skills	Pronunciation	Reading Skills
Welcome page 2	• Meet your classmates • Learn about yourself • Learn about *Project Success*				
1 **Diana Helps Out** page 5	• Talk about things in common • Talk about things I have seen and done • Offer to help someone	• Coordination with *too, so, either,* and *neither* • Simple past and present perfect	• Read a work schedule	• Word stress: highlighting the important words • Using stress and intonation to contrast and correct information	• an article about government control over foods and drinks **Reading Skill:** • Read for the main idea
2 **Ben Makes Plans** page 19	• Describe recent activities • Ask for a promotion • Ask for help	• Present perfect and present perfect continuous • *Would rather* and *would prefer*	• Read a pay stub	• Stressed syllables in words ending in *-tion* and *-ity* • Relaxed pronunciation of *could you* ("couldja") and *would you* ("wouldja")	• an article offering advice on getting a promotion **Reading Skill:** • Identify supporting details
3 **Lena's Bad Day** page 33	• Describe a traffic accident • Accept criticism • Explain why I can't achieve a goal	• Past perfect • Gerunds as subjects and objects	• Read a street map	• Pronunciation of *-ed* endings • Weak pronunciation of *can* and *will*	• an article offering advice on what to do after a car accident **Reading Skill:** • Make predictions
4 **Sam Keeps His Cool** page 47	• Talk about job duties • Discuss work benefits • Remain polite and professional	• Tag questions • *It + be +* adjective *+* infinitive	• Read a medicine label	• Intonation of tag questions • Weak pronunciation of *t* in negative contractions	• an article about parking apps **Reading Skill:** • Make inferences
5 **Emily's Opinions** page 61	• Talk about diet and exercise • Plan an event • Express personal values	• *Should, ought to,* and *had better* • Future continuous	• Read a medical history form	• Weak pronunciation of *to* in *have to* ("hafta") and *ought to* ("oughta") • Silent syllables	• an article about health problems related to too much sitting **Reading Skill:** • Determine the author's purpose

Vocabulary Listening and Speaking Pronunciation	Practical Skills Grammar Reading	Writing Job-Seeking	Unit Tests Midterm Tests Final CASAS Test Prep

Writing Skills	Vocabulary ActiveTeach	Job-Seeking Skills	Career Pathways	CASAS Highlights	Common Core College and Career Readiness
• Write a biographical statement • Use time words and phrases	• Understand prefixes **Learning strategy:** • Recognize negative meanings Word list page 157	• Assess my job needs	• Negotiate • Function under pressure • Prioritize tasks • Ask for help • Help others	0.1.2, 0.1.3, 0.1.4, 0.1.8, 0.2.4, 4.1.6, 4.1.9, 4.6.3, 4.8.2, 6.7.1, 7.1.4, 7.2.6, 7.3.1, 7.3.4, 7.4.4, 7.5.4, 7.7.3, 7.7.4	R. 1, 2, 3, 7, 10 W. 3, 4, 5, 7 SL. 1, 2, 4, 6 L. 1, 2, 4, 6
• Write a description • Use descriptive adjectives	• Understand suffixes **Learning strategy:** • Group by meanings Word list page 157	• Assess my job skills	• Promote yourself • Exhibit self-confidence • Communicate clearly • Ask for help • Help others • Be self-aware	0.1.2, 0.1.3, 0.1.4, 0.1.7, 0.2.1, 0.2.4, 2.8.7, 4.1.8, 4.1.9, 4.2.1, 4.4.1, 4.4.2, 4.4.5, 4.4.7, 4.5.7, 5.4.4, 7.1.1, 7.1.3, 7.2.6, 7.4.4, 7.7.3, 7.7.4	R. 1, 2, 4, 5, 10 W. 4, 5, 7 SL. 1, 3, 4, 6 L. 1, 2, 4
• Write a narrative • Use place words and phrases (*between, behind, in front of*, etc.)	• Understand word roots **Learning strategy:** • Avoid interference when learning new words Word list page 158	• Research job ads	• Empathize / show concern • Accept criticism • Learn from mistakes • Show resilience • Deal with difficult situations • Sell an idea	0.1.2, 0.1.3, 0.1.4, 0.1.6, 0.1.8, 1.9.7, 2.2.1, 2.2.5, 4.1.3, 4.1.6, 4.4.4, 4.6.1, 4.6.4, 4.7.3, 4.8.3, 4.8.4, 4.8.6, 6.7.1, 7.2.4, 7.4.4, 7.5.3, 7.7.3	R. 1, 2, 3, 7, 8, 10 W. 3, 4, 5, 7 SL. 1, 2, 3, 6 L. 1, 2, 4, 6
• Write a letter of complaint • Understand the structure of a letter of complaint	• Use suffixes to change nouns into adjectives **Learning strategy:** • Use suffixes Word list page 158	• Network with friends and online	• Mentor others • Stress the positives in a situation • Communicate a complaint • Deal with difficult situations • Demonstrate persistence and perseverance • Network	0.1.2, 0.1.3, 0.1.4, 0.1.6, 0.1.7, 3.1.6, 3.3.2, 3.3.4, 3.4.5, 4.1.3, 4.4.4, 4.8.2, 4.8.5, 7.2.4, 7.4.4, 7.7.3, 7.7.4	R. 1, 2, 4, 8, 10 W. 1, 2, 4, 5, 7 SL. 1, 2, 4, 6 L. 1, 2, 3, 4
• Write a business letter • Use a business letter format	• Identify collocations **Learning strategy:** • Make word webs Word list page 159	• Prepare a résumé	• Give advice • Report your progress • Demonstrate organizational skills • Influence / persuade others	0.1.2, 0.1.3, 0.1.4, 0.2.4, 3.2.1, 3.5.2, 3.5.9, 3.6.4, 4.1.2, 4.6.2, 4.6.4, 4.7.3, 4.8.7, 6.7.2, 7.1.3, 7.2.6, 7.4.4, 7.5.1, 7.7.3	R. 1, 2, 4, 6, 7, 10 W. 2, 4, 5, 7 SL. 1, 3, 4, 6 L. 1, 2, 3, 4

For complete correlations please visit www.pearsoneltusa.com/projectsuccess

Scope and Sequence 4

Unit	Listening/Speaking VIDEO	Grammar VIDEO	Practical Skills	Pronunciation	Reading Skills
6 **Diana Takes Charge** page 75	• Complain about a bill • Recall details about someone • Take responsibility in a situation	• Present and simple past passive • Adjective clauses	• Read a vehicle registration renewal notice	• Stressed syllables in numbers • Linking a vowel sound to the preceding word	• an article about phone cramming **Reading Skill:** • Scan for specific information
7 **Ben Makes a Difference** page 89	• Talk about volunteer work • Deal with workplace gossip • Talk about financial responsibility	• Placement of direct and indirect objects • Modals of possibility and conclusion	• Read a credit card application	• The reduced vowel /ə/ in unstressed syllables • Weak pronunciation and linking of *of* and *for*	• an interview with a volunteer **Reading Skill:** • Identify cause and effect
8 **Lena Reports** page 103	• Report housing problems • Give a progress report • Call about returning merchandize	• Reported speech: statements and imperatives • Adverb clauses of time	• Read a return policy	• The vowel sounds /æ/ (r<u>a</u>n), /ʌ/ (<u>u</u>p), and /ɑ/ (j<u>o</u>b) • Pausing between thought groups	• an article about renter's rights **Reading Skill:** • Identify pertinent information
9 **Emily's Teamwork** page 117	• Give instructions • Talk about moving • Work as a team	• Phrasal verbs • Adverb clauses of reason	• Read a lease	• Stress in phrasal verbs • Stress in two-syllable words	• an article about parent involvement in education **Reading Skill:** • Identify fact versus opinion
10 **Sam Looks Forward** page 131	• Explore career opportunities • Talk about wishes and dreams • Set goals	• Embedded questions • Present unreal conditional	• Read a course schedule	• Intonation in conditional sentences • Consonant clusters	• an article about how technology changes work / life balance **Reading Skill:** • Interpret the author's point of view

Vocabulary	Practical Skills	Writing	Unit Tests
Listening and Speaking	Grammar	Job-Seeking	Midterm Tests
Pronunciation	Reading		Final CASAS Test Prep

Writing Skills	Vocabulary ActiveTeach	Job-Seeking Skills	Career Pathways	CASAS Highlights	Common Core College and Career Readiness
• Write for a specific audience • Think about your audience	• Look for context clues **Learning strategy:** • Learn words from different meanings in different contexts Word list page 159	• Write a cover letter	• Communicate a complaint • Develop interpersonal relationships • Deal with difficult situations • Think on your feet • Show leadership	0.1.2, 0.1.3, 0.1.4, 0.1.6, 0.1.7, 1.2.5, 1.3.3, 1.6.3, 2.1.2, 2.5.1, 4.1.2, 4.3.2, 4.6.2, 7.2.1, 7.2.2, 7.2.6, 7.4.3, 7.4.4, 7.7.3, 7.7.4	R. 1, 2, 4, 8, 10 W. 1, 2, 4, 5, 7 SL. 1, 2, 3, 6 L 1, 2, 4
• Write a personal note • State your purpose clearly	• Understand metaphors **Learning strategy:** • Write personal sentences Word list page 160	• Prepare for a job interview	• Ask for clarification • Delegate responsibility • Navigate office politics • Communicate ideas clearly • Influence / persuade others	0.1.2, 0.1.3, 0.1.4, 0.1.6, 0.2.3, 1.2.5, 1.3.2, 1.6.2, 1.6.7, 1.8.6, 2.8.9, 4.1.5, 4.8.6, 5.6.5, 7.2.6, 7.2.8, 7.4.4, 7.5.1, 7.7.3, 7.7.4	R. 1, 2, 3, 4, 6, 10 W. 2, 3, 4, 5, 7 SL. 1, 2, 4, 6 L. 1, 2, 3, 5
• Explain a process • Use transition words (*besides, in addition,* etc.)	• Understand synonyms **Learning strategy:** • Use synonyms Word list page 160	• Answer common interview questions	• Deal with difficult personalities • Demonstrate persistence and perseverance • Report your progress • Manage others • Communicate a complaint	0.1.2, 0.1.3, 0.1.4, 0.1.7, 1.2.5, 1.3.1, 1.3.3, 1.4.5, 1.4.7, 1.6.2, 1.6.3, 1.7.3, 4.1.5, 4.1.7, 4.6.4, 4.7.3, 7.2.1, 7.2.6, 7.4.4, 7.7.3, 8.2.6	R. 1, 2, 5, 6, 10 W. 1, 2, 4, 5, 7 SL. 1, 3, 4, 6 L. 1, 2, 5, 6
• Write a comparison-and-contrast paragraph • Use words to express similarities and differences	• Understand antonyms **Learning strategy:** • Use familiar words to learn new words Word list page 161	• Ask questions at a job interview	• Communicate information clearly • Develop interpersonal relationships • Manage stress • Delegate responsibility • Work as a team	0.1.2, 0.1.3, 0.1.4, 0.1.7, 1.4.1, 1.4.3, 1.6.5, 2.8.9, 4.1.5, 4.1.7, 4.6.1, 4.8.1, 4.8.5, 7.4.4, 7.5.4, 7.5.6, 7.6.3, 7.7.3, 7.7.4	R. 1, 2, 3, 6, 8, 10 W. 1, 2, 4, 5, 7 SL. 1, 2, 3, 6 L. 1, 2, 5, 6
• Write a statement of opinion • Use persuasive language	• Recognize word families **Learning strategy:** • Learn words that go together Word list page 161	• Write a follow-up message after a job interview	• Be self-aware • Make informed decisions • Negotiate • Promote yourself	0.1.2, 0.1.3, 0.1.4, 0.1.6, 0.2.4, 1.6.2, 2.8.3, 2.8.7, 4.1.9, 4.4.5, 7.1.1, 7.1.3, 7.2.6, 7.4.4, 7.4.9, 7.6.3, 7.7.3, 7.7.4	R. 1, 2, 6, 9, 10 W. 1, 2, 4, 5, 7 SL. 1, 2, 4, 6 L. 1, 2, 3, 5, 6

To the Teacher

Project Success is a dynamic six-level, four-skills multimedia course for adults and young adults. It offers a comprehensive and integrated program for false-beginner to low-advanced learners, with a classroom and online curriculum correlated to national and state standards.

KEY FEATURES

In developing this course we focused on our students' future aspirations, and on their current realities. Through inspiring stories of adults working and mastering life's challenges, we illustrate the skills and competencies adult English language learners need to participate fully and progress in their roles at home, work, school, and in the community. To create versatile and dynamic learning tools, we integrate digital features such as video, audio, and an online curriculum into one unified and comprehensive course. The result is *Project Success*: the first blended digital course designed for adult-education English language learners.

MULTIMEDIA: INSIDE AND OUTSIDE THE CLASSROOM

All *Project Success* materials are technologically integrated for seamless independent and classroom learning. The user-friendly digital interface will appeal to students who are already technologically adept, while providing full support for students who have less computer experience.

In class, the teacher uses the **ActiveTeach** DVD-ROM to project the lessons on the board. Video, audio, flashcards, conversation frameworks, checklists, comprehension questions, and other learning material are all available at the click of a button. Students use their print **Student Book** as they participate in class activities, take notes, and interact in group work.

Outside of class, students access their *Project Success* **eText** to review the videos, audio, and eFlashcards from class. They use their **MyEnglishLab** access code to get further practice online with new listenings and readings, additional practice activities, and video-based exercises.

A VARIETY OF WORKFORCE AND LIFE SKILLS

Each level of *Project Success* presents a different cast of characters at a different workplace. In each book, students learn instrumental language, employment, and educational skills as they watch the characters interact with co-workers, customers, family, and friends. As students move through the series, level by level, they learn about six important sectors in today's economy: food service, hospitality, healthcare, higher education, business, and retail.

The language and skills involved in daily life range from following directions, to phone conversations, to helping customers, to asking permission to leave early. By representing a day in the life of a character, *Project Success* can introduce a diverse sampling of the content, language, and competencies involved in daily life and work. This approach allows students to learn diverse competencies and then practice them, in different settings and contexts, at different points in the curriculum.

VIDEO VIGNETTES

Each unit is organized around a series of short videos that follow one main character through his or her workday. In Listening and Speaking lessons, students watch the video together, see the character model a key competency in a realistic setting, and then practice the competency in pairs and groups. Discussion questions and group activities encourage students to identify and interpret the rich cultural content embedded in the video. The unit's grammar points are presented in the context of natural language in the video and then highlighted for more study and practice in a separate grammar lesson.

CRITICAL THINKING SKILLS

In the *What do you think?* activity at the end of nearly every lesson, students analyze, evaluate, infer, or relate content in the lesson to other contexts and situations.

A ROBUST ASSESSMENT STRAND

The series includes a rich assessment package that consists of unit review tests, midterms, and a CASAS-like final test. The tests assess students on CASAS objectives which are integrated into practical skills and listening strands.

The tests are available online or in a printable version on the ActiveTeach.

THE COMPONENTS:

ActiveTeach

This is a powerful digital platform for teachers. It blends a digital form of the Student Book with interactive whiteboard (IWB) software and printable support materials.

MyEnglishLab

This is a dynamic, easy-to-use online learning and assessment program that is integral to the *Project Success* curriculum. Original interactive activities extend student practice of vocabulary, listening, speaking, pronunciation, grammar, reading, writing, and practical skills from the classroom learning component.

eText

The eText is a digital version of the Student Book with all the audio and video integrated, and with a complete set of the pop-up eFlashcards.

WELCOME TO *PROJECT SUCCESS*!

Project Success is a six-level digital and print English program designed for you. It teaches English, employment, and learning skills for your success at work and school.

YOUR CLASSROOM LEARNING

Bring the Student Book to your classroom to learn new material and to practice with your classmates in groups. Every unit has:

- Three video-based lessons for your listening and speaking skills
- One practical skills lesson
- Two grammar lessons
- One lesson for getting a job
- One lesson for writing
- One lesson for reading
- One review page

YOUR ONLINE LEARNING

Your access code is on the front cover of your Student Book. Use the access code to go online. There you will find eText and MyEnglishLab.

Go to your eText to review what you learned in class. You can watch the videos again, listen to audio, and review the Vocabulary Flashcards.

Go to MyEnglishLab online to practice what you learned in class. MyEnglishLab has:

- Extra listening practice
- Extra reading practice
- Extra grammar practice
- Extra writing practice
- Extra practice of vocabulary skills
- Extra practice of life skills
- Additional video-based exercises
- "Record and compare," so you can record yourself and listen to your own pronunciation
- Instant feedback
- Job-seeking activities

Welcome Unit

MEET YOUR CLASSMATES

A ◀))) **Listen and read the conversation.**

Carlos: Hi. My name is Carlos.

Nadia: Hi. My name is Nadia. Nice to meet you.

Carlos: Nice to meet you, too. Where are you from, Nadia?

Nadia: Turkey. What about you?

Carlos: I'm from Colombia.

Nadia: Oh! How long have you been here?

Carlos: Three years. I came here when I finished school.

Nadia: Wow! You speak English very well.

Carlos: Thank you, but I need to study more.

Nadia: Well, I've been a student here for a year now. It's an excellent school. You'll learn a lot here.

Carlos: Great! I think you speak well, too. Why are you studying English?

Nadia: I'm planning to go to college. I'm going to apply next year.

Carlos: That's terrific. I'm hoping to get a better job.

B PAIRS **Practice the conversation. Use your own names and information.**

C **Walk around the room. Meet your classmates.**

LEARN ABOUT YOURSELF

A **Take the learning styles survey on page 3.**

B **Count the number of *a*, *b*, and *c* answers. Write the numbers.**

_____ a answers   _____ b answers   _____ c answers

C GROUPS **Discuss your learning styles.**

- If you scored mostly *a*'s, you may have a visual learning style. You learn by seeing and looking.
- If you scored mostly *b*'s, you may have an auditory learning style. You learn by hearing and listening.
- If you scored mostly *c*'s, you may have a kinesthetic learning style. You learn by touching and doing.

Knowing your learning style can help you understand why some things are easier for you than other things.

1. Are you surprised by the results you got? Explain.
2. Do you think knowing your learning style will help you in your class? In what ways?

What's Your Learning Style?

Choose the first answer that you think of. Circle *a*, *b*, or *c*.

1 When I study, I like to _____.
a. read notes or look at diagrams and illustrations
b. repeat information silently to myself
c. write notes on cards or make diagrams

2 When I listen to music, I _____.
a. picture things that go with the music
b. sing along
c. tap my feet

3 When I solve a problem, I _____.
a. make a list of things to do and check them off as I do them
b. talk about the problem with experts or friends
c. make a diagram of the problem

4 When I read for pleasure, I prefer _____.
a. a travel book with a lot of pictures
b. a novel with a lot of conversations
c. a crime story where you have to solve a mystery

5 When I'm learning to use a computer or new equipment, I prefer _____.
a. watching a DVD about it
b. listening to someone explain it
c. using the equipment and figuring it out for myself

6 The day after a party, I remember _____.
a. the faces of the people I met there, but not their names
b. the names of the people there, but not their faces
c. what I did and said there

7 When I tell a story, I'd rather _____.
a. write it
b. tell it out loud
c. act it out

8 When I'm trying to concentrate, the thing I find most distracting is _____.
a. things I see, like people moving around
b. things I hear, like other people's conversations
c. things I feel, like hunger, worry, or neck pain

9 When I don't know how to spell a word, I will usually _____.
a. write it out to see if it looks right
b. sound it out
c. write it out to see if it feels right

10 When I'm standing in a long line, I usually _____.
a. read a newspaper
b. talk to the person in line in front of me
c. tap my feet and move around

LEARN ABOUT *PROJECT SUCCESS*

A **Learn about your book.**
1. Look at the cover of your book. What's the title?
2. Look at the inside front cover. Find the access code.
3. See page iii. How many units are in your book?
4. Where can you find a list of vocabulary words?

B **Meet the characters in your book.**
They all work at Sundale State University.

I'm Diana Nhan. I'm an administrative assistant to the dean of the Business Department. I like to garden and to cook.

I'm Ben Ramírez. I work at the Records Center. I love soccer—I play every weekend at the park.

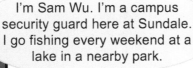

I'm Lena Panich. I'm an Information Technology, or IT, technician. For me, my work is my passion—I like exploring new computer equipment and new software.

I'm Sam Wu. I'm a campus security guard here at Sundale. I go fishing every weekend at a lake in a nearby park.

I'm Emily Campos. I'm a Facilities Manager. I have two teenage sons. I spend a lot of my free time helping with event planning at their school.

1 Diana Helps Out

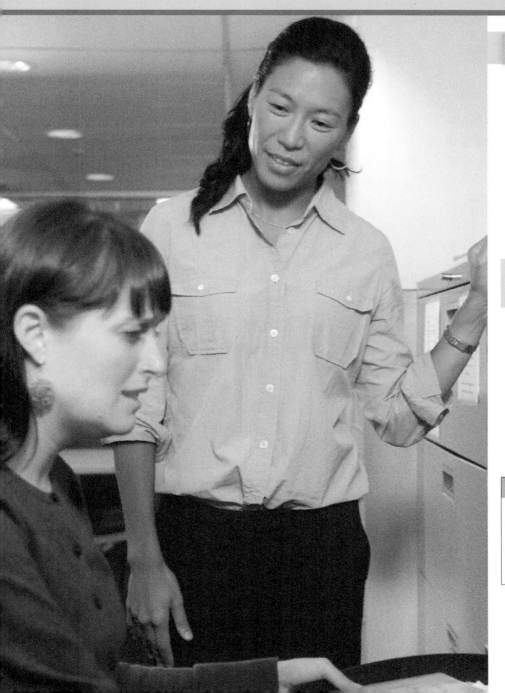

MY GOALS

☐ Talk about things in common

☐ Read a work schedule

☐ Talk about things I have seen and done

☐ Offer to help someone

☐ Assess my job needs

Go to MyEnglishLab for more practice after each lesson.

Diana Nhan
Diana   *Today*
Working at a large university is so interesting! You never know who you're going to meet.

Talk about things in common

 ## GET READY TO WATCH

Diana and Amaya are meeting for the first time.
What do you think they will talk about?

 ## WATCH

A ◼◀ **Watch the video. Was your guess correct?**

B ◼◀ **Watch the video again. Circle the correct answers.**

1. Amaya sits with Diana because _____.
   a. they are friends
   b. they want to talk about movies
   c. the place is crowded

2. Both women like _____.
   a. rainy weather
   b. romantic comedies
   c. the restaurant across the street

3. Diana wasn't planning on going to the basketball game because _____.
   a. she doesn't pay attention to sports
   b. she's going to the movies
   c. her husband wouldn't like it

> **Pronunciation Note**
>
> Important words in a sentence are stressed. They sound longer and louder than other words.
>
> ◀))) **Listen and repeat. Notice the stressed words in the responses.**
>
> I **love** ro**man**tic **com**edies.   I do, **too**.
>
> I **wish** it would **just** get **warm**.   **So** do I.

 ## CONVERSATION

A ◼◀ **Watch part of the video. Complete the conversation.**

Amaya: Have you seen *Last Days in Paris*? Everybody is talking about it.

Diana: Yeah, I went last weekend. It was great. Have you seen it?

Amaya: Not yet, but I want to. I love _____ comedies.

Diana: I do, too.

Amaya: Maybe I'll go this weekend. Going to the big game on Saturday, though.

Diana: Oh, yeah, the basketball game. I don't really _____ sports.

Amaya: Neither do I, usually. But this is our team, and they're in the finals!

B PAIRS **Practice the conversation.**

C PAIRS **Practice the conversation again. Make similar conversations. Talk about movies, sports, or other things you may have in common.**

WHAT DO YOU THINK?

PAIRS Diana and Amaya are making small talk because they've just met. What topics are appropriate for small talk? What topics are *not* appropriate for small talk?

GRAMMAR

2

Coordination with *too*, *so*, *either*, and *neither*

 STUDY **Coordination with *too*, *so*, *either*, and *neither***

Too / Either

Diana **likes** to garden, and Amaya **does, too**.
Diana **doesn't like** sports, and Amaya **doesn't either**.

So / Neither

Diana **is** an assistant, and **so is** Amaya.
Diana **is not** a big sports fan, and **neither is** Amaya.

Grammar Note

In conversation, the more informal *me, too* and *me, neither* are common.

PRACTICE

A **Complete each sentence.**

1. Amaya will support the school team, and so _____will_____ Diana.

2. They didn't go to the basketball game, and neither _____ we.

3. I haven't tried the new restaurant, and Maria _____ either.

4. She has seen that movie, and so _____ I.

5. He's going to the game on Saturday, and we _____, too.

6. Sal didn't go to the game, and Paula _____ either.

B **On a separate piece of paper, combine the sentences into one, using *too*, *so*, *either*, or *neither*.**

1. Richard follows sports. Tom follows sports.

> Richard follows sports, and Tom does, too.
> Richard follows sports, and so does Tom.

2. Jun doesn't like gardening. Maria doesn't like gardening.

3. Abed hasn't worked here long. Chong Li hasn't worked here long.

4. Diana ate lunch in her office yesterday. Amaya ate lunch in her office yesterday.

5. Tania can't come to the reception. Ravi can't come to the reception.

6. The dean will come to the meeting. The Activities director will come to the meeting.

WHAT ABOUT YOU?

PAIRS Talk to your partner and find six things you have in common. Then meet with another pair and share what you learned.

Kim enjoys playing soccer, and so do I.

GET READY

Diana's friend Ted is a security guard at the university. Look at the work schedule for the week of February 17 to February 23. Why do employers post work schedules like this?

PRACTICAL READING

A Read the schedule posted in the Security Office. Match the terms and definitions.

SUNDALE UNIVERSITY
Work Schedule—Week of February 17 – 23

Shift	Monday	Tuesday	Wednesday	Thursday	Friday	Saturday	Sunday
Day 8 A.M.– 4 P.M.	Yaniv / Jane	Yaniv / Jane	Ted / Jane	Ted / Jane	Ted / Jane	Ted / Yaniv	Ted / Yaniv
Swing 4 P.M.– 12 A.M.	Miranda / Anna	Miranda / Kwame	Anna / Kwame	Miranda / Anna	Miranda / Kwame	Anna / Kwame	Anna / Kwame
Night 12 A.M.– 8 A.M.	Rico / Olga	Rico / Olga	Bao / Olga	Bao / Olga	Bao / Olga	Bao / Carlos	Bao / Carlos

Vacation days—Rico: February 19 to February 23

_____ **1.** day shift

_____ **2.** swing shift

_____ **3.** night shift

_____ **4.** vacation days

a. a period of work usually from around midnight to 8:00 A.M.

b. days when an employee is away from work and still gets paid

c. the typical period of work at most jobs, usually from 8:00 A.M. to 4:00 P.M. or 9:00 A.M. to 5:00 P.M.

d. a period of work usually from around 4:00 P.M. to midnight

B Read the schedule again. Answer the questions.

1. Which shift does Ted usually work?

2. Which shift does Bao usually work?

3. Which guard will be on vacation this week?

4. Which guard usually works with Ted during the day shift on weekdays?

5. Which guard usually works with Ted during the day shift on weekends?

6. Which guards (other than Ted) work on February 20 and February 21?

C GROUPS Ted needs to be away from Wednesday night, February 19, to Friday evening, February 21. Which guards can Ted ask to cover his shift? Who is your first choice? Why? Who are your other choices? Compare your answers with the other groups.

PRACTICAL SPEAKING

 A ◀)) **Ted is trying to switch shifts with another guard. Listen and read the conversation.**

Ted: Hi Rico! Can you do me a favor?

Rico: Maybe. What is it?

Ted: I have to go to my nephew's wedding. Could I switch shifts with you on Thursday and Friday?

Rico: I'm sorry. I can't switch with you. I'm visiting my cousins on those days!

B PAIRS **Practice the conversation.**

C PAIRS **Look at the schedule again. Role play a similar conversation between Ted and another guard. Give a good reason if the other guard can't switch shifts with Ted.**

PRACTICAL LISTENING

◀)) **Listen to this podcast about one problem night shift workers may face. Circle the correct answers.**

1. According to the CDC, what percent of employed adults in the United States reported getting fewer than six hours of sleep?
   a. 13   **b.** 30   **c.** 40

2. How many hours of sleep should a healthy adult get every night?
   a. five to seven
   b. six to eight
   c. seven to nine

3. Which type of night shift workers are more likely to get less sleep?
   a. convenience store clerks
   b. security guards
   c. truck drivers

4. Why do night shift workers have more problems sleeping?
   a. Their environments are too noisy during the day.
   b. It's harder to stay asleep when the human body is warm during the day.
   c. Physical needs, such as hunger and thirst, make it harder to stay asleep during the day.

5. What is the CDC recommending that companies do?
   a. They should change schedules for night shift workers so they can get more sleep.
   b. They should pay night shift workers more.
   c. They should hire fewer night shift workers.

WHAT DO YOU THINK?

GROUPS Imagine you're a night shift worker. What can you do to get more sleep?

LESSON

4

Talk about things I have seen and done

GET READY TO WATCH

Diana couldn't find a file folder. What do you think happened?

WATCH

A ◼◖ **Watch the video. Was your guess correct?**

B ◼◖ **Watch the video again. Read the statements. Circle *True* or *False*. Correct the false statements.**

1. Diana misplaced a green file folder.	True	False
2. Diana took the folder into the break room.	True	False
3. Paula once put a folder in the refrigerator.	True	False
4. Paula finds Diana's folder in the copy room.	True	False
5. Diana is worried because Mark wants the folder this afternoon.	True	False
6. Mark took the folder from Diana's drawer.	True	False

CONVERSATION

A ◼◖ **Watch part of the video.
Complete the conversation.**

Paula: What's the matter, Diana? Did you lose something?

Diana: Yes! Have you seen a blue _____ folder?

Paula: I don't know. What kind of folder?

Diana: It's just an _____ folder, but it's bright blue. You can't miss it.

Paula: I think I saw it on your desk this morning.

Diana: I know it was on my desk this morning, but it's not here now!

Paula: Did you take it anywhere today?

Diana: I took it into the copy room, but I've already looked in there. It's not there.

B PAIRS **Practice the conversation. Use your own names.**

C PAIRS **Practice the conversation again. Make similar conversations. Talk about finding something you lost.**

> **Pronunciation Note**
>
> When we contrast or correct information, we use stress and intonation (the way the voice goes up and down) to make the words we are contrasting stand out.
>
> ◀)) **Listen and repeat.**
>
> It was on my desk this **mor**ning, but it's not here **now**.
>
> That's a **yel**low folder. I'm looking for a **blue** folder.

WHAT DO YOU THINK?

PAIRS Even though Mark didn't ask for the file, Diana tells him that she misplaced it. Was this a good idea? Why or why not?

LESSON 5 GRAMMAR

Simple past and present perfect

STUDY Simple Past and Present Perfect

Simple Past	Present Perfect
I **saw** it two hours ago.	**I've seen** it many times.
He **didn't finish** the work yesterday.	He **hasn't finished** the work yet.
Did you **see** the folder this morning?	**Have** you **seen** the folder?
Where **were** you last night?	Where **have** you **been**?

Grammar Note

- Use the simple past to talk about a specific time in the past.
- Use the present perfect to talk about an unspecified time in the past.

PRACTICE

A **Circle the correct form. If either form is possible, circle the present perfect.**

It's 3:00 P.M., and so far today Diana (1) was / (has been) very busy in the Dean's Office. This morning, as usual, she (2) checked / has checked the dean's schedule. Then a faculty member (3) called / has called. He had something important to discuss with the dean, so Diana (4) rearranged / has rearranged the schedule. Since then, she (5) answered / has answered 15 emails about the conference the dean is planning. Also, she (6) called / has called several of the conference participants. Last week she (7) made / has made arrangements with a hotel for the out-of-town guests, but she (8) didn't choose / hasn't chosen the caterer yet.

B **Complete the questions about yourself, using the verbs in parentheses.**

1. _____Have you seen_____ (see) any good movies lately?
2. _____ (misplace) anything recently?
3. How many jobs _____ (have) in your lifetime?
4. When _____ (take) your first English class?
5. _____ (eat) anything yet today?
6. How long _____ (study) at this school?
7. _____ (read) any good books lately?

C **Write your own responses to the questions in Exercise B. If possible, add specific information.**

Yes, I have. I saw Last Days in Paris last week.

WHAT ABOUT YOU?

PAIRS Work together to write four questions in the simple past and four in the present perfect. Ask about music, sports, and/or travel. Find a new partner and ask your questions. Answer your partner's questions with specific information.

Read for the main idea

GET READY

Diana grows her own vegetables and is very concerned about the food she eats.
Are you careful about what you eat?

READ

◀))) **Listen and read the article. Do you think a government should control
what people eat and drink? Why or why not?**

You Can't Have That!

Imagine a very hot day in July. You work in a state government building. You go to the vending machine to get soda, but then you remember that the government has banned sugary drinks.

It's not the law everywhere, but more and more government officials are deciding what their citizens eat and drink . . . or do not eat and drink. The soft drink story isn't complete fiction. In San Francisco, sodas and other sweet drinks were banned from vending machines in public buildings, and the governor replaced them with diet sodas and soy milk. The mayor of New York City wanted to stop the sale of large sodas, and politicians in Philadelphia wanted people to pay an extra tax for those same sugary drinks.

The restrictions aren't limited to drinks. California and New York City have rules that no restaurants can serve food with trans fats—that's over 88,000 restaurants in California! Children in certain cities and states are affected, too. Texas has state laws limiting junk food in schools. New York City has a wellness policy that stopped school bake sales. It also limits food choices in vending machines. City supervisors in San Francisco have banned toys from being included with meals in fast food restaurants.

Why has the government started making these rules? They were made in the name of health. Substandard eating habits have led to obesity. Obesity is related to other medical problems, such as heart disease, strokes, and diabetes. In 2010, the number of obese people was over 30 percent in 12 states. As the obesity numbers rise, so do the medical costs. Health care costs more for an obese person than for people of average weight. Those costs are shared by all taxpayers—not just the heavy ones.

Despite the government's goal of healthier living, some people disagree with the bans and want to overturn the few rules the government has in place. They believe it is a right to be able to choose what they want to eat. Parents feel it is their responsibility, and not the government's, to decide what their children eat. Yet, the eventual savings to skyrocketing insurance costs seems to outweigh the fact that a government official is taking away the 16-ounce soft drink.

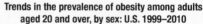

**Trends in the prevalence of obesity among adults
aged 20 and over, by sex: U.S. 1999–2010**

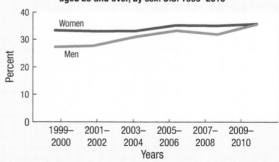

Source: Data from the Centers for Disease Control and Prevention, 2012.

AFTER YOU READ

A **Read the Reading Skill. Read the article again. Circle the main idea.**

a. Poor eating habits have led to medical problems for many people.

b. The government has a right to tell its citizens what to eat and drink.

c. Some local governments are banning certain foods and drinks to encourage healthy living.

d. Not everyone agrees that the government should be making food and drink decisions.

Reading Skill

The **main idea** of an article is the most important idea. Sometimes it is in the first paragraph of the article. Each paragraph also has its own main idea.

B **Look at the graph in the article. Read the statements. Circle *True* or *False*. Correct the false statements.**

1. In 1999–2000, more men were obese than women.   True   False

2. In 1999–2000, more than 30% of men were obese.   True   False

3. In 2009–2010, the percentage of obese men was almost the same as that of obese women.   True   False

4. From 1999–2000 to 2009–2010, the percentage of obese men increased a lot.   True   False

5. From 1999–2000 to 2009–2010, the percentage of obese women increased a lot.   True   False

VOCABULARY STUDY   Prefixes

Build Your Vocabulary

A **prefix** is a group of letters that is added to the beginning of a word to change its meaning and make a new word. Some common prefixes are *dis-*, *sub-*, and *out-*.

Prefix	Definition	Example
dis-	shows an opposite	disagree (= not agree)
sub-	shows something is not as good	substandard (= below standard)
out-	shows something is greater than	outweigh (= be more important than)

Read the Build Your Vocabulary note. Complete the sentences with the words from the chart.

1. Some controls are good because _____ eating habits can lead to obesity and other medical problems.

2. Not all people _____ with the government bans because they want health care costs to be lower.

3. For some state governments, healthy living and lower insurance costs _____ personal choices of food.

WHAT DO YOU THINK?

GROUPS Which is more important—lower health care costs or freedom to make your own choice? How much control do you think a government should have over its people?

ON THE WEB

For more information about this topic, go online and search "food regulations" and the name of your city. Report back to the class.

Write a biographical statement

GET READY

The university staff newsletter includes a "Meet the Newest Staff Member" article—a short biography of that person. What kind of information do you expect to find in a biography?

STUDY THE MODEL

 Read the biographical statement. What did the writer choose to highlight about the person?

Meet the Newest Staff Member!

Miguel Lopez was born in a small town in Mexico in 1987. He is the son of a farmer and an elementary school teacher and has three younger sisters— Sara, Ana, and Rosa. His family still lives in Mexico. It was hard for him to leave, but Miguel moved to southern California in December of 2005 because he wanted to try new things.

Miguel's first goal was to find a job, and in January of 2006, he got a job at a construction company. At first, he worked as a crew member, but he learned very quickly. In 2008, he got a promotion and became the foreman of a crew. His other goal was to study English. He started studying English at night at Sundale Community Education in 2008. At that time, he knew a little English. He finished all six levels of English in only four years. While studying at Sundale Community Education, Miguel met his wife, Luz, and they got married in 2011. Then, he finished his last English class in 2012. Miguel continued working for the construction company until the end of 2013 when he saw a job opening in the Office of Campus Development at Sundale State University. At that time, he thought his experience in construction could be helpful as the university prepares to grow over the next ten years. The director agreed, and Miguel will manage the scheduling of construction teams to improve our campus buildings and build new ones.

When he isn't working, Miguel likes spending time at the beach and going dancing with Luz. He is also learning to surf. Luz works in education, too; she is a secretary for a local high school. They love living in Sundale. They enjoy traveling and are saving their money to take a vacation to New York City next year.

> **Writing Tip**
>
> Writers use **time words and phrases** in biographical statements. These time words make the writing easier to understand.

 Read the Writing Tip. Read Miguel's biographical statement again. Underline the time words and phrases.

C **Look at and complete the timeline the writer used to plan his/her writing.**

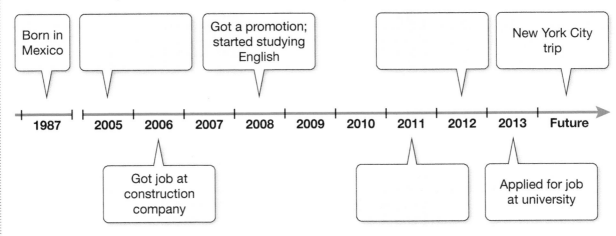

Born in Mexico

Got a promotion; started studying English

New York City trip

1987 | 2005 | 2006 | 2007 | 2008 | 2009 | 2010 | 2011 | 2012 | 2013 | Future

Got job at construction company

Applied for job at university

BEFORE YOU WRITE

You're going to write a biographical statement about yourself or a family member. Use the timeline to plan your statement.

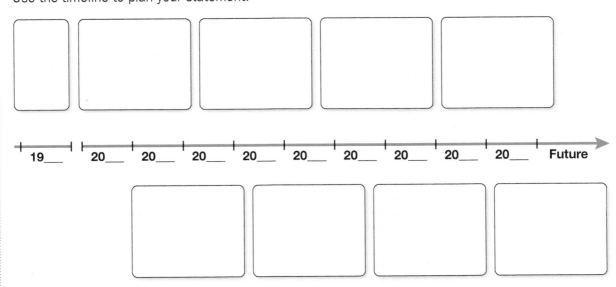

19___ | 20___ | 20___ | 20___ | 20___ | 20___ | 20___ | 20___ | 20___ | 20___ | Future

WRITE

Review the Model and the Writing Tip on page 14. Use the ideas from your timeline to write your biographical statement.

LISTENING AND SPEAKING

Offer to help someone

GET READY TO WATCH

Paula looks worried and unhappy. What is her problem? What do you think Diana is saying?

WATCH

A ◼◀ Watch the video. Were your guesses correct?

B ◼◀ Watch the video again. Answer the questions.

1. Why did Paula get behind on her work?
2. Why does Diana offer to help Paula?
3. What does Diana do for Paula?
4. What advice does Diana give Paula?
5. Why does Paula like to make lists?
6. What does Paula show Diana when she comes back?

CONVERSATION

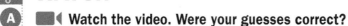

A ◼◀ Watch part of the video. Complete the conversation.

Diana: How are you doing, Paula? You look a little _____.

Paula: I am! I was out for two days, and everything just _____ up.

Diana: Can I help you with anything?

Paula: Oh, thank you, but I know you have your own work to do . . .

Diana: It's OK. I've got some time on my hands. What do you need?

Paula: I need to call in this _____ order. I need to fax these documents. I'm not sure what that is . . .

Diana: I can take care of the supply order for you.

Paula: That would help a lot. Thanks!

B PAIRS Practice the conversation. Use your own names.

C PAIRS Practice the conversation again. Make similar conversations. Talk about things you need help with.

WHAT DO YOU THINK?

PAIRS Does Diana give Paula good advice? How does prioritizing help? What else can Paula do to catch up on her work?

JOB-SEEKING SKILLS

Assess my job needs

@RafikAramayan *Today*
My friend Diana told me about a job opening at Sundale University. I'm looking for a job because my previous company moved.

GET READY

Before Rafik starts looking for a job, he has to assess his needs.
For example, he may need to work full-time. What other things may he need?

ASSESS JOB NEEDS

Rafik made a chart to help him assess what type of job would meet his needs. Look at the chart. Read the statements. Circle *True* or *False*. Correct the false statements.

My Next Job			
What I Want	**Absolutely Necessary**	**Preferred**	**Not So Important**
Full-time	✓		
Programming job		✓	
Close to home			✓
Day shift			✓
Health benefits		✓	
Paid vacations		✓	
Higher or same salary		✓	
Bonuses			✓

1. Rafik really wants to be able to work close to his home.   True   False
2. He thinks that it is very important that his next job is a full-time job.   True   False
3. He may work as a computer salesperson at a computer store if he can't get a job as a programmer.   True   False
4. He cannot accept a job on the night shift.   True   False
5. He will only accept a job that has health benefits and paid vacations.   True   False
6. He'd like to make more money than he did at his last job, but he will take a job that pays less money.   True   False

PUT YOUR IDEAS TO WORK

A On a separate piece of paper, make a chart to help you assess your own job requirements and preferences. Use Rafik's chart as a model. Add any other factors that you want to include in the first column. Place one checkmark [✓] for each row.

B PAIRS Look at each other's charts. Explain why you filled out your chart the way you did. Listen to your partner's explanation.

UNIT 1 REVIEW

 GRAMMAR

In this unit, you studied:

- Coordination with *too, so, either,* and *neither*
- Simple past and present perfect

See page 145 for your Grammar Review.

VOCABULARY See page 157 for the Unit 1 Vocabulary.

Vocabulary Learning Strategy: Recognize negative meanings

A **Find words from the list that have negative meanings and write them here.**

awful _____ _____ _____

_____ _____ _____

_____ _____ _____

B **Circle 5 words in Exercise A. Write a sentence with each word.**

SPELLING See page 157 for the Unit 1 Vocabulary.

CLASS Choose 10 words for a spelling test.

LISTENING PLUS

A **Watch each video. Write the story of Diana's day on a separate piece of paper.**

Diana meets a new friend at lunch time. Her name is Amaya. She works in
the Activities Office.

B **PAIRS Review the conversation in Lesson 4 (see page 10). Role play the conversation for the class.**

NOW I CAN

PAIRS See page 5 for the Unit 1 Goals. Check ☑ the things you can do. Underline the things you want to study more. Tell your partner.

> I can _____. I need more practice with _____.

2 Ben Makes Plans

MY GOALS

- ☐ Describe recent activities
- ☐ Ask for a promotion
- ☐ Read a pay stub
- ☐ Ask for help
- ☐ Assess my job skills

Go to MyEnglishLab for more practice after each lesson.

Ben Ramírez

Ben   *Today*

I've been thinking about my career lately, and I'm ready for the next step.

19

Describe recent activities

 GET READY TO WATCH

Ben sees an old friend on his way back to work. What do you think they are saying to each other?

 WATCH

A ◼◀ Watch the video. Was your guess correct?

B ◼◀ Watch the video again. Read the statements. Circle *True* or *False*. Correct the false statements.

1.	Ben hasn't seen Ahmed for ten years.	True	False
2.	Ben and Ahmed went to Sundale University together.	True	False
3.	Ahmed has already been accepted to the MBA program.	True	False
4.	Ahmed has less education than Ben.	True	False
5.	Ben has to pay 75% of his tuition.	True	False
6.	Ben got married recently.	True	False

 CONVERSATION

A ◼◀ Watch part of the video. Complete the conversation.

Ahmed: I haven't seen you since City College. What have you been up to?

Ben: Well, I've been working here at the university. And for the last year I've been taking courses towards a business _____.

Ahmed: Really? I'm thinking about starting the _____ program in the fall.

Ben: Have you already applied?

Ahmed: Yep. I got my _____ letter last week. I'm just here to check this place out and pick up some information at the Registrar's Office. Where do you work?

Ben: I'm in the Records Office.

B PAIRS Practice the conversation.

C PAIRS Practice the conversation again. Make similar conversations. Talk about what you've been doing and what you are doing now.

Pronunciation Note

In words that end in *-tion* or *-ity*, we stress the syllable just before *-tion* or *-ity*.

◀)) **Listen and repeat.**

promótion   congratulátions

univérsity   responsibílity

redúction

WHAT DO YOU THINK?

PAIRS Ahmed is starting an MBA program because he's about to become a father, and he wants to take care of his family. Do you think it is a good idea for him to go back to school now? Why or why not?

GRAMMAR

2 Present perfect and present perfect continuous

 STUDY Present Perfect and Present Perfect Continuous

Present Perfect	Present Perfect Continuous
I've **taken** several classes.	I've **been working** here for a few years.
They **haven't seen** each other for a long time.	He **hasn't been playing** soccer lately.
Have you **finished** your MBA?	**Have** you **been taking** business classes?

Grammar Note

- Use the present perfect to describe an action that was completed at an indefinite time in the past.
- Use the present perfect or the present perfect continuous to describe an action that began in the past and continues to the present.
- Remember that non-action verbs (see p. 155) cannot be continuous.

PRACTICE

A **Circle the correct form of the verb. Use the present perfect continuous if the action is continuing.**

1. Ahmed (hasn't seen) / hasn't been seeing Ben since City College.

2. Ben has studied / has been studying business for two years.

3. Ben hasn't gotten / hasn't been getting married yet.

4. Ben has won / has been winning a lot of soccer games lately.

5. Ben hasn't asked / hasn't been asking his boss about the promotion yet.

6. Ahmed has already received / has already been receiving his acceptance letter.

B **Complete the paragraph with the present perfect or the present perfect continuous. Use the present perfect continuous if the action is continuing.**

It takes four years for a full-time student to complete a BA at Sundale University.

Ben _____*hasn't been studying*_____ full-time. He _____ two
           1. not study   2. take

classes every semester for the last three years. He _____
                                        3. already / finish

all of the general business classes, and he can now start management classes.

He _____ to studying management because that's the area
        4. look forward

he's most interested in. He _____ to start his own business.
                             5. always / want

WHAT ABOUT YOU?

PAIRS Quickly make a note of four things you have done several times and four things you have been doing lately. Share your ideas with a partner. Then find a new partner and talk about what your first partner has done/has been doing.

3

Identify supporting details

GET READY

Ben wants a promotion. What advice would you give to people who want to advance in their careers?

READ

🔊 **Listen and read the article. Does any of the advice sound familiar to you?**

Getting to the Next Rung

Do you want a new challenge at work? Do you want to take the next career step? Don't wait. Be an activist! Career experts agree there are actions employees can take to get promoted. If you're ready to climb the ladder, then keep reading.

Talk to your boss about your desire to do well and grow with the company. Talking about your goals is smart because bosses usually like interested and confident employees. Plus, bosses know about opportunities in the company. If they don't know, they can find out. Chances are they have been with the company longer than you. They can teach you the skills needed to get a promotion.

Volunteer for more work. Ask your boss for additional tasks or help coworkers with theirs. You can also volunteer for committees. Some companies have committees that plan social events, community service, or business strategies. There are two purposes of volunteering. First, you prove you are a team player. Second, you learn additional skills that make you valuable.

Improve communication skills. It's not only about talking; it's about listening, too. People who listen are usually liked by colleagues and bosses. Those skills make you a "people person." Since you are so appealing to others, you are likely to be considered for promotions.

Be creative. Everyone is able to think of the "same old thing." Try to think of ideas that are unusual. Not only will you stand out, but your boss will, too. Creative solutions sometimes make companies more money and, as a result, lead to promotions for the innovative thinkers.

Keep studying. Take classes that will develop professional skills. For example, enroll in a writing or management course. Go to conferences that will teach you about the field. Read books about your job. If you know the new trends, then you may well become one of the "go to" people.

In general, work hard! Meet all of your deadlines and beat them if you can. In the end, there is no one way to be promoted. The best advice is to combine more than one strategy; then it might not be as long as you think to reach the next rung.

Reading Skill

Details in a reading support the main idea and important points the writer is making. Look for **supporting details** such as facts, statements, names, numbers, and examples to help you understand what the writer thinks is important.

AFTER YOU READ

Read the Reading Skill on page 22. Read the article again. Circle the best answers.

1. Which statement supports the idea that volunteering for more work is important?
   a. It shows your boss that you are interested and confident.
   b. It shows that you are a team player.
   c. It shows that you are a people person.

2. Which statement supports the idea that communication skills help you get promoted?
   a. They help the company make more money.
   b. They make you more appealing to others.
   c. They show you are a "go to" person.

3. Which statement supports the idea that creativity is an important skill to have?
   a. It helps you stand out.
   b. It teaches you the new trends.
   c. It makes you more likeable.

4. Which statement supports the idea that continuing to study is good?
   a. It proves you are an innovative thinker.
   b. It helps you meet all of your deadlines.
   c. It develops your professional skills and teaches you about the field.

VOCABULARY STUDY Suffixes

Build Your Vocabulary

A **suffix** is a group of letters that is added at the end of a word to form a new word. A suffix can change the part of speech. Some common suffixes are *-ist* and *-able*.

-ist: (noun) the doer of an action
-able: (adjective) capable of doing something

Add *-ist* or *-able* to words that end in consonants:
novel + ist = novelist
break + able = breakable

Drop *-e* and then add *-ist* or *-able* to words that end in *-e*.
cycle – e + ist = cyclist
advise – e + able = advisable

Read the Build Your Vocabulary note. Change the words into nouns with *-ist* or adjectives with *-able*.

-ist		-able	
active	_____	value	_____
guitar	_____	accept	_____
journal	_____	wash	_____
cartoon	_____	comfort	_____

WHAT DO YOU THINK?

PAIRS Which piece of advice from the reading do you think is the best? Why? Can you add any other advice? Be prepared to share your advice with the class.

ON THE WEB

For more information about this topic, go online and search "promotion advice." Find one good tip and report back to the class.

LISTENING AND SPEAKING

Ask for a promotion

GET READY TO WATCH

Ben is asking his boss for a promotion.
What do you think he will say to persuade her?

WATCH

A ■◀ **Watch the video. Was your guess correct?**

B ■◀ **Watch the video again. Answer the questions.**

1. Why has Ben been doing a lot more work lately?

2. What job does Ben want?

3. Why can't Karen give Ben the job he wants?

4. What does Karen offer Ben instead?

5. What is Ben going to email to Karen?

6. What does Ben give to Karen?

CONVERSATION

A ■◀ **Watch part of the video. Complete the conversation.**

Ben: Will you be posting the Administrative Coordinator position soon?
I would like to be considered.

Karen: Unfortunately, Ben, I can't post the position because of the _____ cuts.

Ben: I see.

Karen: I think I can promote you to Assistant III, though. That won't change your

_____, but it will raise your salary some.

Ben: OK, thank you. I'd rather be an Assistant III than an Assistant II!

Karen: I'll need to write a letter making the _____. Do you have an updated résumé?

Ben: Yes, I do. I can print it out for you right away.

B PAIRS **Practice the conversation. Use your own names.**

C PAIRS **Practice the conversation again.**
Make similar conversations.

WHAT DO YOU THINK?

PAIRS Ben doesn't get the promotion he wants, but he does get a raise. Why do you think
Karen offered him a raise? Should he have pushed harder for a promotion? Why or why not?

Would rather and *would prefer*

 STUDY *would rather* and *would prefer*

would rather

Ben **would rather**	work	in the front office.	
He**'d rather**		in the front office	**than** in the back office.

would prefer

Ben **would prefer**	**to work**	in the front office.	
He**'d prefer**	**the job**	in the front office	**to** the job in the back office.

Questions

Would you **rather work** in the front or in the back?
Would you **prefer** an email or a printed copy?

Grammar Note

- *Would prefer* can also be followed by a gerund: *Ben would prefer working in the front office.*
- When comparing with *would rather*, use *than*.
- When comparing nouns with *would prefer*, use *to* between the nouns.

PRACTICE

A **Circle the correct words.**

1. I'd prefer look / (to look) for a new job.
2. I'd rather talk to the supervisor now to / than wait until later.
3. I'd prefer a raise to / than a new job title.
4. I'd prefer / rather to work in a different office.
5. She had / would rather answer the phones.
6. He'd rather / prefer work with computers than with people.

B **On a separate piece of paper, write questions with *would rather* or *would prefer*, using the words in parentheses.**

1. (work in an office / work outside)

   > Would you rather work in an office
   > or work outside?

2. (a busy office / a quiet office)

3. (talk to customers / work on the computer)
4. (high salary / good benefits)
5. (use a computer / fix things)
6. (a job you love / a job that pays very well)

C PAIRS **Ask and answer the questions in Exercise B.**

WHAT ABOUT YOU?

GROUPS Write ten verbs on index cards or small pieces of paper. Mix them up and put them face down on the table. Take turns drawing a card and making a sentence with *would rather* or *would prefer*, using the verb on the card.

I would rather go to a movie than go shopping.

GET READY

Ben gets an email from an old friend who is taking classes at Kingston Community College. What do you think the email will talk about?

STUDY THE MODEL

A **Read the email. What does the writer describe?**

To: B_ramirez@sundale.edu
Subject: My impressions of KCC

Hi Ben,

Well, I started classes at Kingston Community College this week. You would love the peaceful campus. We're not far from St. Louis, but it's very quiet here. I feel like I am in the country. The campus is surrounded by grassy fields that are full of colorful wildflowers. Near the student center there's even a beautiful pond with a cute family of ducks.

The university buildings are modern and well designed. The classrooms all have huge windows, so it's always bright. Maybe that's a bad thing. I probably spend too much time in class looking out of the windows instead of taking notes! There are interactive whiteboards in every classroom, with high-speed Internet access. The teachers can put the textbook on the board and just click on it to play the audio and video files. They can even use the board to show us websites on the Internet. The only problem has been the air-conditioning. It hasn't been working all week, and the classrooms are so hot.

Everyone here is very friendly. The students come from all over the world. We have different backgrounds, but we all get along very well. I've already made some new friends. An interesting guy from Korea invited me to a party this Saturday. It's going to be fun. The teachers are great. They're very patient and helpful. They do assign a lot of homework, though. Last night I didn't go to bed until 1:00 A.M. I had so much to do!

Take care!

Emilio

> **Writing Tip**
>
> Writers use a lot of **descriptive adjectives** when they are describing something. An adjective is a word that describes a noun or pronoun. These make writing more interesting and paint a picture for the reader.

B **Read the Writing Tip. Read the campus description again. Underline the adjectives. Circle the nouns and pronouns the adjectives describe.**

c **Look at the word wheel the writer used to plan his writing and complete it.**

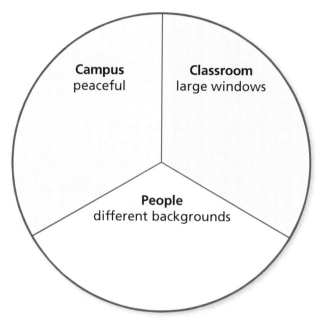

BEFORE YOU WRITE

You're going to write a description of your school. Use the word wheel below to plan your description.

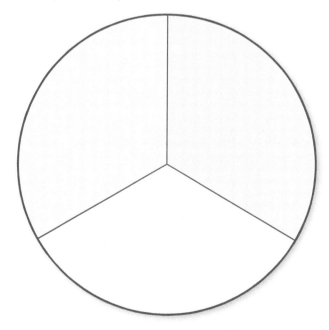

WRITE

Write a description of the campus, classrooms, and people of your school. Review the Model and the Writing Tip on page 26. Use the ideas from your word wheel to write your description.

GET READY

Ben's colleague Brian is checking his pay stub to make sure his pay is correct.
Do you receive a pay stub? Do you get a paper pay stub or do you view it online?

PRACTICAL READING

 A

Look at Brian's pay stub. How much money did Brian get for this pay period after all taxes and other deductions?

Sundale University 100 University Blvd Southern California, CA						Earnings Statement	
EMPLOYEE NO. 045345	EMPLOYEE NAME Brian Greene		SOCIAL SECURITY NUMBER XXX-XX-9898	PERIOD BEGINNING 02/16/2014	PERIOD END 03/01/2014	CHECK DATE 03/04/2014	
EARNINGS	HOURS	RATE	CURRENT AMOUNT	WITHHOLDINGS/DEDUCTIONS		CURRENT AMOUNT	YEAR TO DATE
Regular Pay Overtime Pay	80.00 7.60	25.45 35.75	2036.00 271.70	STATE TAX FEDERAL TAX FICA-OASDI FICA-HI		87.69 281.54 96.92 33.46	386.91 1120.38 384.46 141.57
GROSS PAY 2307.70	CURRENT DEDUCTIONS 499.61		NET PAY 1808.09	YTD EARNINGS 9325.45	YTD DEDUCTIONS 2033.32	YTD NET PAY 7292.13	CHECK NO. 89744

B **Read Brian's pay stub again. Circle the correct answers.**

1. When did Brian get paid?
   a. February 16, 2014   b. March 1, 2014   c. March 4, 2014

2. How often does Brian get a paycheck?
   a. every week   b. every two weeks   c. every month

3. How much state tax was deducted from Brian's pay for this pay period?
   a. $281.54   b. $87.69   c. $194.46

4. How much state tax has been deducted from Brian's pay this year?
   a. $386.91   b. $1,120.38   c. $499.61

5. What is Brian's regular hourly pay rate?
   a. $35.75 per hour   b. $80 per hour   c. $25.45 per hour

6. How many hours of overtime was Brian paid for during this pay period?
   a. 7.60 hours   b. 80 hours   c. 0

7. What is usually the largest deduction from Brian's pay?
   a. the state tax   b. the federal tax   c. FICA—OASDI

8. How much money has Brian earned so far before all deductions?
   a. $7,292.13   b. $2,307.70   c. $9,325.45

C PAIRS Do you check your pay stubs for mistakes? Why or why not? Have you ever found a mistake on your pay stub? If so, how did you fix the problem?

PRACTICAL SPEAKING

A 🔊)) **Brian is talking to Amy, a Human Resource clerk, about his pay stub. Listen and read the conversation.**

Brian: Can I speak to you for a minute?

Amy: Sure. What's up?

Brian: I don't think I got paid correctly. I worked 13 hours of overtime— 7 hours two weeks ago and 6 hours last week.

Amy: Let me check your time card. I'll take a look and let you know what I find.

Brian: Thanks!

B PAIRS **Practice the conversation.**

C PAIRS **Role play a similar conversation between Brian and the Human Resource clerk. Talk about a different problem. Choose one of the following situations: Brian didn't get "illness" pay for a day on which he was sick. Brian didn't get paid for two vacation days.**

PRACTICAL LISTENING

🔊)) **Listen to the news program about tax tips. Answer the questions on a separate sheet of paper.**

1. What could be bad about getting a very large federal tax refund?

2. What is one way to reduce the amount of federal tax that is withheld from your paycheck every pay period?

3. What form do you use to tell the federal government how many personal allowances you are claiming?

4. When do most employees get a W-4 form?

5. How can you get a new W-4 form if your personal situation changes during the year?

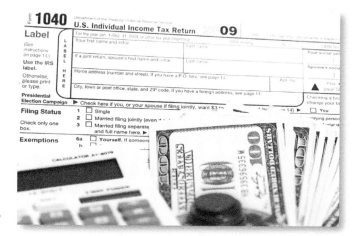

WHAT DO YOU THINK?

PAIRS Would you prefer a larger federal tax refund at tax time or a larger paycheck every pay period? Why?

Ask for help

GET READY TO WATCH

Ben is having problems with a machine. Have you had similar experiences? How can you find help?

WATCH

 ◀ Watch the video. Circle the correct answers.

1. Ben is having trouble with the machine because _____.
   a. it's new, and he missed the training
   b. Rochelle is using the machine
   c. he can't use it as a scanner

2. The machine wasn't working because _____.
   a. he didn't clear the paper jam
   b. he didn't save the file
   c. he didn't press "reset"

3. Ben's going to call Lena to _____.
   a. send out an email
   b. schedule a makeup training
   c. arrange for Tom's training

CONVERSATION

 A **◀ Watch part of the video. Complete the conversation.**

Ben: Rochelle. I'm sorry to _____ you, but could you help me with something?

Rochelle: I can try. What is it?

Ben: I'm having trouble with the new copier.

Rochelle: Sure. I can help you with that.

Ben: Thanks a lot. Would you mind showing me how to clear a paper _____?

Rochelle: Not at all. I'll be with you in just a second.

B PAIRS Practice the conversation. Use your own names.

C PAIRS Practice the conversation again. Make similar conversations. Ask for help on how to do certain things.

Pronunciation Note

The voice usually goes up at the end of polite requests. Notice that in conversation, we often pronounce *could you* as "couldja" and *would you* as "wouldja."

◀)) **Listen and repeat.**

Could you **help** me with something?

Would you mind showing me how to clear a **pa**per jam?

WHAT DO YOU THINK?

PAIRS Is it reasonable for Ben to ask Lena to schedule a new training? Why or why not?

JOB-SEEKING SKILLS

Assess my job skills

@RafikAramayan *Today*
Putting my skills down on paper has really helped me feel confident about myself and my abilities.

GET READY

Rafik was a computer programmer at his previous job. What skills do you think Rafik has?

ASSESS JOB SKILLS

**Rafik made a chart to help him assess his skills. Look at the chart.
Read the statements. Circle *True* or *False*. Correct the false statements.**

Self-Assessment of Job Skills				
Job-Specific Skills	**Excellent**	**Good**	**OK**	**Not so good**
Programming languages—Java, C++, PHP	✓			
Website construction and maintenance			✓	
Lead a software development group	✓			
Build a database				✓
Transferable Skills	**Excellent**	**Good**	**OK**	**Not so good**
Communication with other employees	✓			
Leadership skills	✓			
Takes initiative	✓			
Budget management				✓
Goal setting		✓		
Problem solving	✓			

1. Rafik thinks he has excellent programming skills in Java, C++, and PHP.   True   False

2. Rafik thinks that he would be able to solve most problems that he would face at work.   True   False

3. Rafik doesn't like to work with other programmers.   True   False

4. Rafik feels that he is very good at his database skills.   True   False

5. Rafik rated his ability to manage a project budget as better than average.   True   False

6. Rafik thinks that his leadership skills, problem-solving skills, communication skills, and his ability to take initiative will be useful in any job.   True   False

PUT YOUR IDEAS TO WORK

A   **Make a Self-Assessment Chart of your own. List skills in the "Job-Specific Skills" section based on your own education and job experience. List skills in the "Transferable Skills" section that you think are important for any job. Place a checkmark [✓] in one column to rate each skill.**

B   **PAIRS Show each other your self-assessments. Explain your self-assessment to your partner. Discuss with your partner the types of jobs that match your skills. Now do the same thing with your partner's self-assessment.**

GRAMMAR

In this unit, you studied:

- Present perfect and present perfect continuous
- *Would rather* and *would prefer*

See page 146 for your Grammar Review.

VOCABULARY See page 157 for the Unit 2 Vocabulary.

Vocabulary Learning Strategy: Group by meanings

A Choose words from the list and put them into these groups.

College	Job	Pay Stub	Technology
degree	promotion	deductions	flash drive

B Circle 5 words in Exercise A. Write a sentence with each word.

SPELLING See page 157 for the Unit 2 Vocabulary.

CLASS **Choose 10 words for a spelling test.**

LISTENING PLUS

A Watch each video. Write the story of Ben's day on a separate piece of paper.

> On his way back to work, Ben sees Ahmed, an old friend. They haven't seen each other for a long time. It is a wonderful surprise.

B PAIRS **Review the conversation in Lesson 8** (see page 30). **Role play the conversation for the class.**

NOW I CAN

PAIRS **See page 19 for the Unit 2 Goals.** Check ☑ the things you can do.
Underline the things you want to study more. Tell your partner.

> I can _____. I need more practice with _____.

3 Lena's Bad Day

MY GOALS

- ☐ Describe a traffic accident
- ☐ Read a street map
- ☐ Accept criticism
- ☐ Explain why I can't achieve a goal
- ☐ Research job ads

Go to MyEnglishLab for more practice after each lesson.

Lena Panich

Lena   *Today*

As a computer tech, I work all over campus. Sometimes that's a challenge!

DO NOT USE

Describe a traffic accident

 GET READY TO WATCH

Lena just saw a traffic accident. Has this ever happened to you? How did it make you feel?

WATCH

 Watch the video. Answer the questions.

1. Where did the accident happen?
2. Where was Lena when the accident happened?
3. What did the SUV do?
4. How much was each car damaged?
5. How did Lena offer to help?
6. What did both drivers do after the accident happened?

CONVERSATION

A **Watch part of the video. Complete the conversation.**

Lena: I just saw an _____ on Pioneer Boulevard.

Marcos: What happened?

Lena: I was headed north on Pioneer, and there was a car right in front of me,

a small _____. It was going through the intersection— it had gotten halfway through when

this SUV _____ right into it.

Marcos: The SUV ran a red light?

Lena: Oh, yeah. Our light had just turned yellow when the sedan went into the intersection.

Marcos: Wow.

B PAIRS **Practice the conversation.**

C PAIRS **Practice the conversation again. Make similar conversations. Describe a traffic accident. Use your own ideas.**

Pronunciation Note

We pronounce the -ed ending on verbs as an extra syllable /ɪd/ only after the sound /t/ or /d/. After other sounds, we pronounce -ed as /t/ or /d/.

Listen and repeat.

-ed = /t/	smashed	looked	stopped
-ed = /d/	happened	turned	damaged
-ed = /ɪd/	headed	decided	expected

WHAT DO YOU THINK?

PAIRS Lena offered to be a witness. Would you do the same thing in her situation? Why or why not?

STUDY Past Perfect

Statements
The light **had** just **turned** yellow when the car entered the intersection.

Questions	Answers
Had the drivers **gotten out** of their cars before the ambulance arrived?	Yes, they **had**.
What **had** Marcos **heard** before Lena got to work?	He **had heard** sirens.

> **Grammar Note**
> - Use the past perfect to show that one action happened earlier than another.
> - The past perfect is more common in written English than in spoken English.

PRACTICE

A **Complete the paragraph. Use the past perfect of the verbs.**

I was driving on Oak Street when a car turned in front of me from a side street.

The driver ___*hadn't seen*___ me because there was a van parked on the corner.
　　　　　　　1. not see

He _____ so quickly that I couldn't avoid hitting him. I looked for witnesses,
　　　2. turn

but no one _____ the accident. Fortunately, the insurance company
　　　　　3. see

determined it was the other driver's fault. I _____ down Oak Street
　　　　　　　　　　　　　　　　　　4. drive

hundreds of times before. But since then, I have avoided that street.

B **Complete each sentence. Write one verb in the simple past and the other verb in the past perfect.**

1. The police officer ___*asked*___ us if we ___*had exchanged*___ insurance information.
　　　　　　　　ask　　　　　　　　　exchange

2. Fortunately, the pedestrian _____ when the car _____ into the crosswalk.
　　　　　　　　　　　　cross　　　　　　　　　drive

3. The insurance company finally _____ back to me after I _____ them three times.
　　　　　　　　　　　　get　　　　　　　　　　call

4. When the accident _____, he was very relieved that he _____ his children that day.
　　　　　　　　happen　　　　　　　　　　　not bring

5. How long _____ you _____ the car before the accident _____?
　　　　　　　　　　own　　　　　　　　　　　happen

6. I _____ that intersection was dangerous, so I _____ very careful there.
　　hear　　　　　　　　　　　　　be

WHAT ABOUT YOU?

PAIRS Take a moment to draw or make notes about a car accident (imaginary or from your experience). Describe the accident to your partner. Use the simple past and the past perfect.

GET READY

Lena uses an online map to show Marcos where she saw the accident.
Have you ever used an online map to find a location or get directions?

PRACTICAL READING

A

**Look at the online street map. What features does an online map
have that a traditional paper street map does not?**

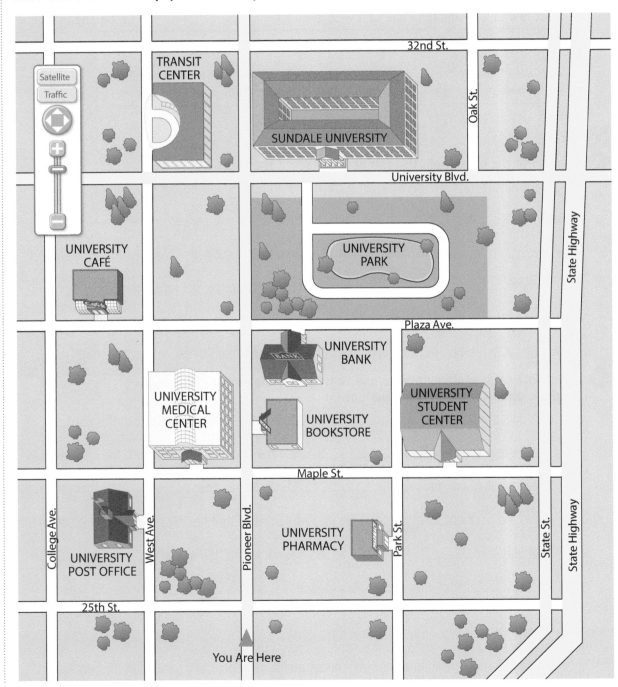

B **Look at the map again. Read the statements. Circle *True* or *False*.
Correct the false statements.**

1.	Sundale University is east of State Highway.	True	False
2.	There is a park across the street from Sundale University.	True	False
3.	The Transit Center is on the northeast corner of West Avenue and University Boulevard.	True	False
4.	The University Café is north of the university.	True	False
5.	The University Student Center is down the street from the University Medical Center.	True	False
6.	The University Bank is around the corner from the University Bookstore.	True	False

PRACTICAL SPEAKING

A ◀))) **A tourist is asking a police officer for directions. Listen and read the conversation.**

Tourist: Excuse me, officer. Can you tell me how to get to the Transit Center from here?

Officer: Sure. Go straight for three blocks. Turn left onto University Boulevard. Walk another block. The Transit Center is on your right, at the corner of University and West.

Tourist: OK! I need to walk straight for three blocks and turn left onto University.

Officer: That's right.

Tourist: Then I walk to the corner of University and West. The Transit Center is on my right.

Officer: You got it.

B PAIRS **Practice the conversation.**

C PAIRS **Look at the map again. Ask your partner for directions to a place on the map. Repeat the directions to confirm. Switch roles.**

PRACTICAL LISTENING

◀))) **Listen to the radio advertisement. Complete the sentences with words from the box. You won't use all the words.**

west	east	northeast	southeast	northwest
southwest	damage	shuttle	insurance	replacement

1. The three locations of 32nd Street Auto Body are the _____ corner of 32nd Street and West Avenue, the _____ corner of 32nd Street and Pioneer Boulevard, and on 32nd Street just _____ of the State Highway.

2. The body shop works with all _____ companies.

3. The body shop will provide you with a _____ vehicle while they are repairing your car.

4. The body shop's _____ drivers will pick you up when your vehicle is ready.

WHAT DO YOU THINK?

PAIRS When was the last time you used a traditional paper map or an online map? What type of maps do you use more often? Do you prefer traditional paper maps or online maps? Why?

Accept criticism

GET READY TO WATCH

Lena is falling behind on her work. Has this ever happened to you? How did you feel? What did you do about it?

WATCH

■◀ **Watch the video. Read the statements. Circle *True* or *False*.**
Correct the false statements.

1. Lena has been working on the projection system at the conference center.	True	False
2. Tom is unhappy because Lena hasn't finished the projection system.	True	False
3. The Dean's Office wants Lena to finish the projection system.	True	False
4. Marcos is having trouble with the upgrade.	True	False
5. Tom needs to spend more time training Marcos.	True	False
6. Lena apologizes to Tom and makes him a promise.	True	False

CONVERSATION

A ■◀ **Watch part of the video.**
Complete the conversation.

Tom: Training Marcos is one of your

_____.

Lena: I know. I need to spend a little more time working with him.

Tom: You really should. It will save you time in the long run.

Lena: That's true.

Tom: Can you _____ the schedule so that he has more time to work with you?

Lena: Yes, I can. I'll have him come over here now. We can plan on finishing the projection system tomorrow.

> **Pronunciation Note**
>
> Words like *can* and *will* usually have a weak pronunciation with a short, unclear vowel sound when they come before another word. At the end of a sentence, they have a strong pronunciation, with a clear vowel sound.
>
> ◀))) **Listen and repeat.**
>
> | It can wait until tomorrow. | I suppose it can. |
> |---|---|
> | It will save you time. | It will. |

B PAIRS **Practice the conversation.**

C PAIRS **Practice the conversation again. Make similar conversations.**
Talk about other job responsibilities and ways to improve.

WHAT DO YOU THINK?

PAIRS Why didn't Lena tell her boss that she was falling behind on her work?
Should employees ask their supervisor for help at the first sign of trouble?
Or should they try to solve the problems themselves? Why?

LESSON **GRAMMAR**

5

Gerunds as subjects and objects

STUDY **Gerunds as Subjects and Objects**

Gerunds as Subjects

Upgrading these computers isn't easy.
Rearranging your schedule is a good idea.

Gerunds as Objects

He's planning on **coming** in early tomorrow.
She's excited about **starting** the new job.

Grammar Note

- A gerund used as the subject of a sentence is always singular.
- Use a gerund after a preposition.

See page 155 for a list of verbs + prepositions + gerunds (*plan on coming*) and adjectives + prepositions + gerunds (*excited about starting*).

PRACTICE

 A Circle gerunds used as subjects. Underline gerunds used as objects. Remember that not all *-ing* forms are gerunds.

(Working) as a computer tech can be very interesting. Keeping up with new technology is a challenge. This job is great for people who are interested in learning and solving problems. One downside to the job is that using a keyboard all day can be bad for your hands and your back. Taking breaks, standing, and walking are essential for protecting your body. Using a good chair is also important.

 B On a separate piece of paper, write a sentence with a similar meaning, using the words in parentheses and the gerund form of the underlined verb.

1. Lena can fix computers. (good at)

   > Lena is good at fixing computers.

2. It's interesting to learn about new software. (fun)

   > Learning about new software is fun.

3. Paula won't drive in the rain. (afraid of)

4. Marcos wants to get a new job. (think about)

5. It's not easy to install computer systems. (difficult)

6. Lena wants to see the movie. (excited about)

7. Lena is going to take her son to visit colleges next weekend. (plan on)

8. It's not safe to drive without a seatbelt. (a bad idea)

WHAT ABOUT YOU?

GROUPS Individually, write eight statements about yourself or expressing an opinion. Use gerunds as subjects in four statements and gerunds as objects in four statements. In groups, take turns reading your statements. Make a checkmark [✓] next to statements that everyone in the group agrees with.

Learning new things is fun. / I'm good at fixing things.

GET READY

Lena reads an article about what to do after a car accident. Look at the title. What advice do you think the article gives?

READ
◀))) **Listen and read the article. Were your guesses correct?**

A CRASH COURSE
Know What to Do After the Crash

Drivers know traffic rules and traffic signs. They have learned how to drive carefully and prevent accidents. But accidents still happen. Unfortunately most people don't know what they should do then. Do you? Read these six tips to make sure you're prepared.

1. Don't leave. When accidents happen, you may get scared and want to drive away. But don't! You should never leave the scene of the accident. Even if you think the accident is your fault, leaving is worse. In fact, it's a crime, and people who "hit and run" could receive tough punishments.

2. Check whether everyone is OK. You may be worried your car is badly damaged, but worry about people first. You should make sure you're not hurt and then check on everyone else—your passengers, the other driver, and passengers in other vehicles. If someone is hurt, call for medical help.

3. Make calls and file reports. If no one is hurt, call the police. The police will file an accident report that might be useful when filing insurance claims.

4. Talk to the other driver. You need to share information. Make sure to exchange names and contact information. Also make sure to get the other driver's insurance details and driver's license number. You should even write down the license plate number. Don't feel bad about this because they'll be writing down your details, too.

5. Don't apologize! One of the biggest mistakes people make is apologizing for the accident. Don't ever say "I'm sorry." Apologizing may make you legally responsible and you may learn that it wasn't your fault . . . even when you think it is.

6. Take pictures. These days many people have a smartphone with a built-in camera. Use it to record the damages and the accident scene. There is no such thing as too much documentation, and photographs help support the factual information.

With accidents numbering in the millions every year, it is very important to know what to do after an accident. Hopefully accidents won't happen. But keep this list in your glove compartment anyway, just in case you need it.

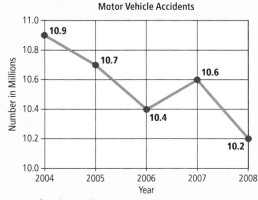

Motor Vehicle Accidents

Source: Data from the United States Census Bureau.

AFTER YOU READ

Look at the line graph on page 40. Circle the correct answers.

1. Which year had the most motor vehicle accidents?
   a. 2004   b. 2005   c. 2007

2. Which year had the fewest motor vehicle accidents?
   a. 2006   b. 2007   c. 2008

3. How many motor vehicle accidents were there in 2006?
   a. 10.6 million   b. 10.4 million   c. 10.9 million

4. How many motor vehicle accidents were there in 2005?
   a. 10.2 million   b. 10.4 million   c. 10.7 million

VOCABULARY STUDY Roots

Build Your Vocabulary

Every word has a **root**. The root is the basic part of a word that shows its main meaning. Prefixes can be added before the root. Suffixes can be added after the root. Knowing some common roots will make reading easier and help expand your vocabulary.

Root	Meaning	Example
-vent-	to come	pre + vent = prevent (before + to come = before sth. comes; to stop sth. from coming)
-fact-	to make or do	fact + ual = factual (to do + adjective suffix = sth. done; sth. relating to facts)
-graph-	to write	photo + graph = photograph (light + to write = a picture written [created] by light)

A **Read the Build Your Vocabulary note. Complete the sentences with the words from the box.**

(photograph   prevent   factual)

1. Even if you are a careful driver, you can't always _____ accidents from happening.
2. There are a few _____ errors in the report.
3. I took a _____ of the crowd with my new cell phone.

B **Work with a partner. Think of two or more words with the roots -vent-, -fact-, and -graph-.**

-vent- _____   -fact- _____   -graph- _____

_____   _____   _____

_____   _____   _____

WHAT DO YOU THINK?

PAIRS Read the article again. Which advice do you think is the most valuable? Explain.

ON THE WEB

For more information about this topic, go online and search "car accident advice." Report back to the class.

GET READY

Lena reads about a car accident on someone's blog. What kinds of place words do you expect to see in a narrative of a car accident?

STUDY THE MODEL

A **Read the blog. What did the writer do after the accident happened?**

Home | Recent Posts | Archives | My Links

View My Complete Profile
_____

BLOG ARCHIVE
▼ 2014 (62)
  ▶ March (11)
  ▶ February (23)
  ▶ January (28)
▶ 2013 (259)
▶ 2012 (343)
▶ 2011 (407)
▶ 2010 (383)
▶ 2009 (336)
▶ 2008 (358)
▶ 2007 (113)

Last Friday started just like every other Friday. I went to class first, and then I went shopping for groceries. Then something unusual happened. At around noon I was driving south on Fox Drive between First and Second Streets. I was getting ready to turn into the parking lot next to the Mi Rancho Mexican grocery store when I noticed two cars in front of me.

One car was a blue Mias. It was in the left lane, but it was not driving in a straight line. It was also going very fast—definitely faster than the speed limit. There was a red Caval in the right lane, ahead of the Mias. It looked just like my brother's Caval. It was driving slower. As the Mias came alongside the Caval, it got closer to the Caval—too close! The driver drove across the line and hit the back end of the Caval. I heard a loud crash and saw the Caval go onto the side of the road and hit a tree on the corner of Fox and Second. After the car hit the tree, the driver of the Mias slowed down, pulled onto the side of the road, and stopped.

I wanted to make sure everyone was all right, so I pulled up behind the cars. I called 911 to report the accident, and then I got out of my car and walked the short distance between my car and the accident. The Mias that caused the accident had some damage to the front right side, and the Caval was damaged in the back. The left tail light was broken, and the bumper was dragging along the ground. Luckily, both drivers were OK, but it was really scary.

Writing Tip

Writers use **place words and phrases** to describe locations when they tell a story. These words and phrases help create a picture to go along with the story. Examples of place words and phrases include *between*, *alongside*, *in front of*, and *behind*.

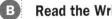 **Read the Writing Tip. Read the blog again. Underline the place words and phrases.**

C **Look at the narrative organizer the writer used to plan his/her story and complete it.**

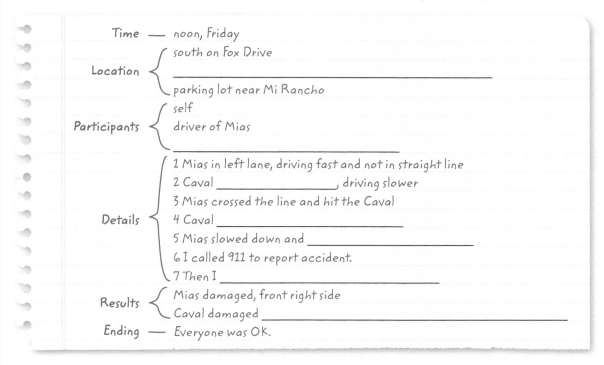

Time — noon, Friday

Location {
south on Fox Drive
_____
parking lot near Mi Rancho
}

Participants {
self
driver of Mias
_____
}

Details {
1 Mias in left lane, driving fast and not in straight line
2 Caval _____, driving slower
3 Mias crossed the line and hit the Caval
4 Caval _____
5 Mias slowed down and _____
6 I called 911 to report accident.
7 Then I _____
}

Results {
Mias damaged, front right side
Caval damaged _____
}

Ending — Everyone was OK.

BEFORE YOU WRITE

You're going to write a narrative about an event you witnessed.
Use the narrative story organizer to plan your narrative.

Time —
Location {
Participants {
Details {
Results {
Ending —

WRITE

Review the Model and the Writing Tip on page 42. Use the
ideas from your narrative organizer to write your narrative.

LISTENING AND SPEAKING

Explain why I can't achieve a goal

GET READY TO WATCH

Lena hasn't finished the work Diana wanted her to do, and Diana is not happy about it. Have you ever had to deal with an unhappy customer? What did you do?

WATCH

■◀ **Watch the video. Answer the questions.**

1. What is Diana concerned about?

2. What has Lena done already?

3. What does she still need to do?

4. What will Lena do if Marcos can't finish the job tomorrow?

5. What can Diana do on Thursday?

6. What can Diana do if there are any last-minute emergencies?

CONVERSATION

A ■◀ **Watch part of the video. Complete the conversation.**

Diana: Hi, Lena. Are you done with the projection system?

Lena: I'm sorry, Diana. I can't finish today.

Diana: Oh, no. I want to be sure all of the technology is running _____ before the conference.

Lena: I know you do. I promise I'll finish it in _____ of time.

Diana: There's going to be a preliminary meeting in here on Friday.

Lena: It will be ready. Marcos will help me.

B PAIRS **Practice the conversation. Use your own names.**

C PAIRS **Practice the conversation again. Make similar conversations. Talk about a job. Explain how the work will be ready on time.**

WHAT DO YOU THINK?

PAIRS Do you think Lena does a good job in dealing with an unhappy customer? Why or why not? Imagine that Diana became angry about the unfinished job. What should Lena do?

JOB-SEEKING SKILLS

Research job ads

GET READY

Rafik found job listings at the Career Center and online. Where else can he find job listings?

RESEARCH JOB ADS

Rafik found several job ads. Read two of the ads Rafik selected and answer the questions.

Game Builders

Game Builders is a leader in the gaming industry. We are looking for an experienced programmer to develop new games for mobile devices. The Game Programmer will work together with artists, designers, and other programmers.

Game Builders provides competitive salaries based on experience, industry competitive benefits, and dedicated support staff. Join our programming team at our new facility in Long Beach, California.

Required Skills & Experience
5+ years of experience in game programming
Experience in game and server programming
Bachelor's degree in Computer Science or a related field

Desired Skills
Experience with mobile platforms and devices
Experience with 3D-content creation software

Note: This is a *part-time* position.

CloseFit
Software Developers Needed

CloseFit is an exciting new company developing an online fitting room, so online customers can see that the clothing they purchase will fit them before they buy it. We're looking for experienced programmers to join our company at our northern California headquarters.

Technical Skills Required:
- Strong programming skills in C++
- Experience with PHP, databases, and website construction

Other Skills Desired:
- Good communication skills, motivated, problem solver
- College degree in computer science or computer engineering
- Versatile team leader who takes initiative

Other Important Information about This Position:
- Full-time / Health benefits and retirement plan
- Paid vacations / Salary based on experience

1. Which of the two jobs is full-time?
2. What type of college degree is required to apply for the position at Game Builders?
3. How many years of experience in game programming is required to apply for the position at Game Builders?
4. If you start working for CloseFit, what type of benefits will you receive?
5. How will your salary be determined if you get the job at CloseFit?

PUT YOUR IDEAS TO WORK

PAIRS Which job listing matches Rafik's needs better? Which matches his skills and experience better? Which job should he apply for? Explain.

GRAMMAR

In this unit, you studied:
- Past perfect
- Gerunds as subjects and objects

See page 147 for your Grammar Review.

VOCABULARY See page 158 for the Unit 3 Vocabulary.

Vocabulary Learning Strategy: Avoid interference when learning new words

A Find words from the list that look or sound similiar and fill in the blanks.

contact	content	plenty	_____
damaged	_____	sedan	_____
competitive	_____	_____	_____
factual	_____	_____	_____

B Circle 5 words in Exercise A. Don't circle words that look or sound similiar. Write a sentence with each word.

SPELLING See page 158 for the Unit 3 Vocabulary.

CLASS **Choose 10 words for a spelling test.**

LISTENING PLUS

A Watch each video. Write the story of Lena's day on a separate piece of paper.

Lena saw an accident on her way to work. An SUV ran a red light and smashed into a car. Luckily, no one was hurt.

B PAIRS **Review the conversation in Lesson 4** (see page 38). **Role play the conversation for the class.**

NOW I CAN

PAIRS **See page 33 for the Unit 3 Goals.** Check ☑ the things you can do. Underline the things you want to study more. Tell your partner.

I can _____. I need more practice with _____.

4 Sam Keeps his Cool

MY GOALS

☐ Talk about job duties

☐ Discuss work benefits

☐ Read a medicine label

☐ Remain polite and professional

☐ Network with friends and online

Go to MyEnglishLab for more practice after each lesson.

Sam Wu

Sam   *Today*
I take my job very seriously, and the benefits are great.

Talk about job duties

GET READY TO WATCH

Sam is explaining the job duties to a new campus security officer. What duties do you think he'll talk about? What does a security officer do?

WATCH

A ◼◀ **Watch the video. Were your guesses correct?**

B ◼◀ **Watch the video again. Read the statements. Circle *True* or *False*. Correct the false statements.**

1. Dennis is on campus for a job interview.	True	False
2. Dennis met Sam on orientation day.	True	False
3. There aren't many serious problems on campus.	True	False
4. There are a lot of bicycle accidents on campus.	True	False
5. Sometimes they give students rides to the parking lot.	True	False
6. Dennis parked in the guest parking area.	True	False

CONVERSATION

A ◼◀ **Watch part of the video. Complete the conversation.**

Sam: So, how do you like the campus so far?

Dennis: I like it. It seems pretty calm. You don't have a lot of problems here, do you?

Sam: Nah, not at all. Once in a while we have to _____ an incident to the city police. We do get a lot of reports about stolen bicycles, though.

Dennis: I see.

Sam: And you have to _____ students not to smoke on campus.

Dennis: But they can smoke in the parking lot, can't they?

Sam: Yes, as long as they're 25 feet from the entrance to any building.

> **Pronunciation Note**
>
> When we add a short question to the end of a sentence, the voice goes up if we are asking a real question to check information. The voice goes down if we are making a comment and expect the other person to agree.
>
> ◀))) **Listen and repeat.**
>
> They can smoke in the parking lot, **can't** they?
> This job is pretty easy, **isn't** it?

B PAIRS **Practice the conversation.**

C PAIRS **Practice the conversation again. Make similar conversations. Talk about a new workplace. Explain the job duties.**

WHAT DO YOU THINK?

PAIRS Sam gives Dennis the impression that his new job won't be difficult. Should he tell Dennis about any problems or difficulties that he may encounter? Why or why not?

STUDY Tag Questions

He's the new security officer,	isn't he?
You weren't parked illegally,	were you?
Sam works in the morning,	doesn't he?
Dennis arrived at the training on time,	didn't he?
He hasn't spent much time on campus,	has he?
Students can't smoke in the buildings,	can they?
They'll see each other often,	won't they?

Grammar Note

- Use tag questions to confirm that information is correct.
- Use negative tags with affirmative statements. Use affirmative tags with negative statements.

PRACTICE

A Complete the sentences with tag questions.

1. The training starts next week, _____doesn't it_____?
2. Dennis likes the campus, _____?
3. There aren't too many problems on campus, _____?
4. Sam and Dennis will work together, _____?
5. Dennis didn't understand the parking signs, _____?
6. The interviews were last week, _____?
7. They see a lot of parking violations, _____?
8. Sam and Dennis have met before, _____?

B On a separate piece of paper, rewrite the regular questions as negative statements with affirmative tag questions.

1. Do we have tennis courts?

   We don't have tennis courts, do we?

2. Is there a lot of crime on campus?
3. Does the student union stay open all night?
4. Will we need our laptops in this class?
5. Did the professor assign homework yesterday?
6. Can I park in the faculty lot?
7. Has the new building opened yet?
8. Was the library open during spring break?

WHAT ABOUT YOU?

PAIRS Write eight tag questions about your partner. Include simple present, simple past, present perfect, future, and questions with modals. Ask and answer each other's questions. The partner who gets the most yes answers is the winner.

Sam and a student discuss parking problems on campus. Where is parking a problem in your community? What makes it difficult?

◀))) **Listen and read the article. In general, do you think electronic apps can solve certain problems?**

Can't Find a Parking Spot? There's an App for That.

Bangalore. Beijing. Buenos Aires. London. Mexico City. Nairobi. New York City. What do these cities have in common? Cities around the world have different foods, customs, and languages. But there is one thing many seem to share—a parking problem.

Frustrated residents in these cities talk of circling blocks for 30, 45, or 60 minutes looking for an open parking space. Some drivers treat the search as a dangerous sport, driving recklessly and fighting with other drivers when a spot appears. Others learn tricks, such as memorizing the street cleaning schedule and grabbing a space the moment the sweeper trucks leave. Drivers in some cities pull trash cans into the street in front of their homes to prevent other drivers from parking there. Sounds ridiculous, doesn't it? There must be another way.

There is. You've heard it time and time again. There's an app for that. Actually, there are now several regional apps available. One is being used in San Francisco. The system uses wireless sensors placed under the streets and in parking garages that indicate when a parking space is available. Within moments, drivers with the app get an alert to their smartphone telling them where they can find an available parking spot. Drivers can see blocks that have a lot of places, marked in blue, and those where no parking is available, marked in red. Sensors are available in over 7,000 metered spots and 12,000 garage spots.

New York City has its own app. Drivers with the app send a message, called a "geo-tagged alert," through the system. The alert lets other drivers know where the newly available parking spot is. It's possible that a new driver can arrive before the first driver has even left the spot. It allows for more careful driving and far less frustration.

Residents of other cities need not despair. Apps are starting or being developed for cities, including Boston, Chicago, Los Angeles, and Seattle. Next time you're upset or wasting time looking for a spot, remember there may be an app to save you the trouble.

Reading Skill

Sometimes writers say things indirectly. You need to use what you read to **make inferences** or logical guesses about what the writer is saying.

AFTER YOU READ

Read the Reading Skill on page 50. Read the article again. Circle the best answers.

1. What does the writer think about the parking problems in New York and San Francisco?
   a. The parking apps made the parking problems better.
   b. The parking apps made the parking problems worse.
   c. The parking apps did not make any difference.

2. How does the writer feel about electronic apps in general?
   a. The writer thinks electronic apps are helpful.
   b. The writer thinks electronic apps are useless.
   c. The writer thinks electronic apps are frustrating.

3. Which of the statements do you think the writer would agree with?
   a. The same parking app can work in different cities.
   b. All parking apps use the same system to find available parking spots.
   c. Parking apps save time and improve driving safety.

VOCABULARY STUDY Changing Nouns into Adjectives

Build Your Vocabulary

Nouns can be changed into adjectives by adding a suffix. Some common suffixes to **change nouns into adjectives** are -al, -ful, -less, and -ous.

Noun	Suffix	Adjective	Noun	Suffix	Adjective
region	-al	regional	wire	-less	wireless
care	-ful	careful	danger	-ous	dangerous

A **Read the Build Your Vocabulary note. Complete the sentences with the adjectives from the chart.**

1. It's _____ to drive and text at the same time.

2. A lot of airports now have free _____ Internet connections.

3. This app only works in certain states in the northeast area. It's a _____ app.

4. Even _____ drivers sometimes cannot avoid accidents.

B **PAIRS Think of more nouns and their corresponding adjectives that end with -al, -ful, -less, and -ous.**

-al   logic: _logical_   _____:_____   _____:_____

-ful   harm: _harmful_   _____:_____   _____:_____

-less   fear: _fearless_   _____:_____   _____:_____

-ous   courage: _courageous_   _____:_____   _____:_____

WHAT DO YOU THINK?

GROUPS Imagine you are a group of city officials. What solution could you offer to your city to help with parking?

ON THE WEB

For more information about this topic, go online and search "parking app" and the name of your city. If there is a smartphone app for your city, tell your class about it.

4

Discuss work benefits

GET READY TO WATCH

Sam and Miranda are discussing job benefits.
What kinds of benefits can you get from a job?
Which are the most important?

WATCH

◀ Watch the video. Answer the questions.

1. Why is Miranda relieved?
2. Why does Sam think it's a good idea to take a vacation?
3. Why didn't Miranda use her vacation days to take care of her daughter?
4. Why can't Miranda go on vacation this year?
5. Why is it hard for Sam to leave this job?
6. What will Sam do after he retires?

CONVERSATION

A **◀ Watch part of the video.
Complete the conversation.**

Sam: I don't know how people get by without good health insurance.

Miranda: Yeah, it's easy to see how you can end up _____ without it.

Sam: And those paid vacation days are important, too!

Miranda: That's true.

Sam: I'm serious! It's really good to get away from work and just relax sometimes. I think it makes me a better worker.

Miranda: You've got a _____.

B PAIRS Practice the conversation.

C PAIRS Practice the conversation again. Make similar conversations. Talk about the importance of job benefits, for example, health insurance, paid vacations, sick leave, and retirement plans.

WHAT DO YOU THINK?

PAIRS Sam has a secure job with good benefits. Should he be thinking about looking for a new job? Imagine you're in the same situation. What would you do? Explain your decision.

It + *be* + adjective + infinitive

 STUDY *it* + *be* + **Adjective** + **Infinitive**

It's hard to pay for health care.
It's not easy to find a job with good benefits.
It's nice to work at a university.
It's wrong to assume that you'll never get sick.
It was depressing to spend the weekend at the hospital.
It might be dangerous to walk to the parking lot alone.

Grammar Note

- It's much more common to use *it* at the beginning of a sentence than to begin a sentence with an infinitive.
- The same idea can be expressed with a gerund subject: *Paying for health care is hard.*

 **PRACTICE**

A **Put the words in the correct order to make sentences.**

1. fun / it's / go / to / swimming   *It's fun to go swimming.*
2. drive / to / in / dangerous / a storm / it's _____
3. to / it's / new things / interesting / learn _____
4. your wallet / to / scary / it's / lose _____
5. lie / relaxing / on / it's / the beach / to _____
6. to / watch / depressing / the news / it's _____
7. it's / buy / to / a house / expensive _____
8. difficult / find / it's / to / the perfect job _____

B **On a separate piece of paper, rewrite the sentences with *It* + *be* + adjective + infinitive.**

1. Going for the job that pays the most is easy.

> *It's easy to go for the job that pays the most.*

2. Paying for your own health insurance is very expensive.
3. Comparing job benefits may be difficult.
4. Thinking about promotions is also important.
5. Learning new things on the job is interesting.
6. Leaving a job can be scary.
7. Meeting new people at work every day is fun.

WHAT ABOUT YOU?

PAIRS Think about what it's like to start a new job or a new school. Write eight sentences with *It* + *be* + adjective + infinitive expressing your opinions about what's difficult, interesting, fun, scary, etc. in these situations. Use a different adjective in each sentence. Share your sentences with a partner and discuss whether you agree or disagree.

GET READY

Sam's friend Franco has been experiencing back pain recently. His doctor gave him a prescription for pain relief medicine. What kind of information do you expect to find on a medicine label?

PRACTICAL READING

Read the medicine label. How should Franco take the medicine?

University Medical Center Pharmacy
415 Maple Street, Long Beach, California 90805

(800) 555-5555

DR. NORMAN MARKS

0043063-03123   Date 03/05/2014

FRANCO GARCIA

TAKE 1 TABLET BY MOUTH EVERY 6 HOURS FOR PAIN.
DO NOT TAKE MORE THAN 4 TABLETS IN 24 HOURS

HYDROCODONE APAP 5 MG/500 MG
20 TABLETS

NO REFILLS – DOCTOR'S AUTHORIZATION REQUIRED

USE BEFORE 01/01/2015

Federal law prohibits the transfer of this drug to any person other than to whom it was prescribed. Avoid alcohol while taking this drug. This drug may cause drowsiness. Use caution while performing tasks requiring mental alertness such as driving. This drug may be habit-forming. Talk to your doctor for medical advice about side effects. Keep this and all other medicines out of the reach of children.

Read the label again. Circle the correct answers.

1. Which statement about Franco's medicine is true?
   a. He can give some of his medicine to another person if that person feels sick.
   b. He can drink alcohol while taking this medicine.
   c. This medicine does not have any side effects.
   d. Before he can get more medicine, his doctor will have to give permission.

2. Which statement about Franco's medicine is NOT true?
   a. He can take one tablet every six hours when he has pain.
   b. He should put the medicine in a place where children can't get it.
   c. He can take up to six tablets in one day.
   d. His medicine can make him sleepy.

3. What should Franco do if he still has medicine left in the bottle in 2015?
   a. Continue to use the medicine until it is used up.
   b. Throw away the medicine in an approved manner.
   c. Give the medicine to someone who can use it.
   d. Give the medicine back to his doctor.

PRACTICAL SPEAKING

A ◀))) **Franco is talking with his doctor. Listen and read the conversation.**

Dr. Marks: Here's the prescription for your back pain.

Franco: Thanks. How do I take it?

Dr. Marks: Take one tablet every six hours with food. Don't take more than four tablets a day.

Franco: So I can take the medicine four times a day.

Dr. Marks: That's right.

Franco: Are there any side effects?

Dr. Marks: You may feel a little tired and sleepy.

Franco: That's not too bad. Thanks, Dr. Marks.

B PAIRS **Practice the conversation.**

C PAIRS **Role play a conversation between a doctor and a patient about a prescription. Talk about how to take the medicine and its side effects. Use the medicine labels below, or use your own ideas.**

TAKE 1 TABLET AFTER EACH MEAL FOR STOMACHACHE
MAY CAUSE DROWSINESS

TAKE 1 TEASPOON EVERY 6 HOURS FOR COUGH
DO NOT TAKE MORE THAN 4 TEASPOONS WITHIN 24 HOURS
MAY CAUSE UPSET STOMACH

TAKE 2 TABLETS TWICE A DAY ON AN EMPTY STOMACH FOR HEADACHE
MAY CAUSE DRY MOUTH

PRACTICAL LISTENING

◀))) **Listen to the news program about prescription pain medicines. Read the statements. Circle *True* or *False*. Correct the false statements.**

1. The leading cause of accidental death in the United States for almost 30 years was prescription pain relievers. True False

2. The leading cause of accidental death in the United States is now motor vehicle accidents. True False

3. There has been an increase in the use of prescription pain relievers in the United States in the last 30 years. True False

4. Very few people who use prescription pain relievers without a doctor's prescription get them from their friends or other family members. True False

5. It is OK to share your prescription medicines with people in your own family. True False

6. It is always a good idea to keep all medicines in a place where children can't get them. True False

WHAT DO YOU THINK?

PAIRS Look at Franco's pain relief medicine label again. Why do you think there are no refills for this medicine? What should Franco do if his back pain doesn't get better after he finishes the medicine?

7 Write a letter of complaint

GET READY

A student in the university writes a letter of complaint about the parking problem on campus and sends it to the editor of the school newspaper. Have you ever read a letter of complaint in the school newspaper?

STUDY THE MODEL

A **Read the letter of complaint. How is it organized?**

Dear Editor:

My name is Peter Lane, and I am a student at Sundale State University. Like most students, I don't live on campus. I am a commuter, and I drive every day from Crestview, which is 20 miles away. When I get to campus in the morning, I can't find a place to park. There are just not enough parking spaces for students. That's a problem.

The parking situation on campus needs to change. First, there are not enough student parking lots. There are only four student lots, but there are five faculty parking lots. There are 15,000 students on campus, but there are fewer than 600 faculty members. Second, there are not enough spaces in the student parking lots. There are more students than spaces, and it takes me at least 30 minutes to find a parking spot. To make things worse, the place I find is usually far away. Sometimes I'm late to class, which is affecting my grades. Third, there is no flexibility with the rules. If I park in a faculty lot, which is closer and has a lot of open spaces, I get a parking ticket from a Campus Security officer. It costs me money that I really need to have to pay my tuition.

I believe there are two possible solutions, and both are easy to implement. I think one of the faculty lots can be converted into a student parking lot. Or, allow faculty and students to share the lots everywhere on campus. Everyone wins!

Sincerely,
Peter Lane

> **Writing Tip**
>
> A **letter of complaint** often has three parts. First, the writer presents a problem. Then the writer gives details about the problem. Finally, the writer suggests a solution.

B **Read the Writing Tip. Read the letter of complaint again. Underline the three supporting details the writer gives about the problem.**

C Look at the outline the writer used to plan his writing and complete it.

A. Problem

    1. describe self

        a. student at Sundale   **b.** _____

    2. describe parking

        a. can't find a place to park   **b.** main problem: _____

B. Details

    1. Not enough student lots

        a. 4 student lots, 5 faculty lots

        b. _____

    2. Not enough spaces in student lots

        a. _____

        b. takes at least 30 minutes to find a spot

    3. No flexibility

        a. _____

        b. costs money

C. Solutions

    1. _____

    2. _____

BEFORE YOU WRITE

A PAIRS **Brainstorm a problem at your school or in your community you'd like to complain about.**

B **Plan your letter of complaint in the outline below.**

A. Problem

    1. describe self

    _____

    2. describe the problem

    _____

B. Details

    1. _____

    2. _____

    3. _____

C. Solutions

    1. _____

    2. _____

WRITE

Review the Model and the Writing Tip on page 56. Use the ideas from your outline to write your letter of complaint.

Remain polite and professional

GET READY TO WATCH

This student is parking in the wrong lot. He's asking Sam not to give him a ticket. Have you ever gotten a traffic ticket? What happened? Did you try to persuade the officer not to give you the ticket?

WATCH

◀ Watch the video. Answer the questions.

1. Why can't the student park in this space?
2. Where is the sign?
3. Why didn't the student park on the other side?
4. Why doesn't the student want to park on Pioneer?
5. What does the student think is outrageous?
6. What finally makes the student move his car?

CONVERSATION

A **◀ Watch part of the video.
Complete the conversation.**

Sam: Sorry, I can't let you park here.

Student: But this lot isn't even full!

Sam: People come and go. These spaces need to be available for _____ when they show up.

Student: Oh, come on, no one's going to notice.

Sam: That's not the point, my friend. Now come on, you need to get moving.

Student: This is ridiculous. I pay a fortune to park here.

Sam: I'm afraid I don't set the parking _____.

B PAIRS **Practice the conversation.**

C PAIRS **Practice the conversation again. Make similar conversations. Talk about behaviors not allowed—for example, smoking on campus, eating in the classroom, and texting during class.**

> ### Pronunciation Note
>
> Negative contractions usually have a strong pronunciation, with a clear vowel sound. But the /t/ sound at the end is often short and quiet. We sometimes drop the /t/ sound altogether when another word follows.
>
> **◀)) Listen and repeat.**
>
> There aren't any spaces left.
>
> I can't let you park here.
>
> This lot isn't even full.

WHAT DO YOU THINK?

PAIRS Do you think Sam behaves in a polite and professional way? Do you think he should just give the student a ticket and walk away? Why or why not?

JOB-SEEKING SKILLS

Network with friends and online

GET READY

In addition to researching job ads, Rafik also signed up at a social networking website that helps people find jobs. How can Rafik use a social network to look for a job?

NETWORK WITH FRIENDS AND ONLINE

Read Rafik's professional profile on an online social network. Read the statements. Circle *True* or *False*. Correct the false statements.

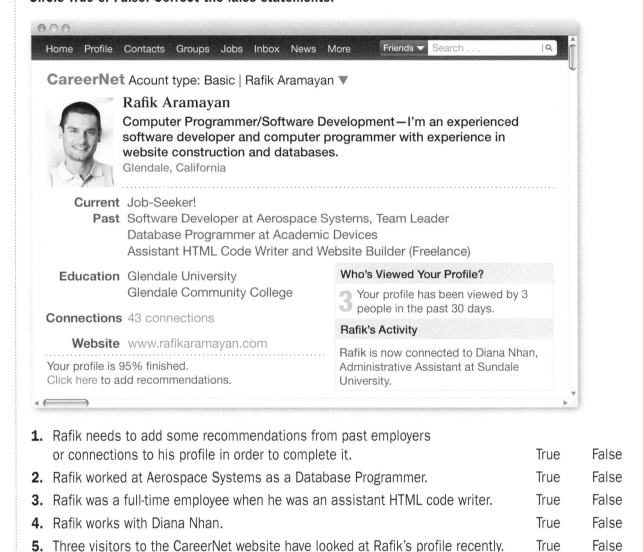

1. Rafik needs to add some recommendations from past employers or connections to his profile in order to complete it.   True   False
2. Rafik worked at Aerospace Systems as a Database Programmer.   True   False
3. Rafik was a full-time employee when he was an assistant HTML code writer.   True   False
4. Rafik works with Diana Nhan.   True   False
5. Three visitors to the CareerNet website have looked at Rafik's profile recently.   True   False

PUT YOUR IDEAS TO WORK

A **This is the one-sentence introduction that Rafik wrote about himself:**
"I'm an experienced software developer and computer programmer with experience in website construction and databases."
Write a one-sentence introduction about yourself.

B **PAIRS** **Read each other's introductions and make suggestions.**

GRAMMAR

In this unit, you studied:

- Tag questions
- *It + be* + adjective + infinitive

See page 148 for your Grammar Review.

VOCABULARY   See page 158 for the Unit 4 Vocabulary.

Vocabulary Learning Strategy: Use suffixes

A Find words from the list that use these suffixes. Put them into these groups.

-ness	-er /-or	-tion

B Circle 5 words in Exercise A. Write a sentence with each word.

SPELLING   See page 158 for the Unit 4 Vocabulary.

CLASS **Choose 10 words for a spelling test.**

LISTENING PLUS

A Watch each video. Write the story of Sam's day on a separate piece of paper.

> *During his morning shift, Sam sees Dennis, a new campus security guard.*
> *It is Dennis's first day. Sam and Dennis discuss some job duties.*

B PAIRS **Review the conversation in Lesson 1** (see page 48). **Role play the conversation for the class.**

NOW I CAN

PAIRS See page 47 for the Unit 4 Goals. **Check ☑ the things you can do. Underline the things you want to study more. Tell your partner.**

> I can _____. I need more practice with _____.

5 Emily's Opinions

MY GOALS

- [ ] Talk about diet and exercise
- [ ] Plan an event
- [ ] Read a medical history form
- [ ] Express personal values
- [ ] Prepare a résumé

Go to MyEnglishLab for more practice after each lesson.

Emily Campos

Emily   Today

I enjoy working with our student helper. She's great, and we learn a lot from each other.

1

Talk about diet and exercise

GET READY TO WATCH

Emily is trying to lose weight. Are there people you know who are also trying to lose weight? What do they do?

WATCH

■◀ **Watch the video. Read the statements.**
Circle *True* or *False*. Correct the false statements.

1. Gina doesn't usually work on this day.	True	False
2. Emily has a work-study job.	True	False
3. Emily isn't eating French fries because she doesn't like them.	True	False
4. Emily is trying to eat less salt.	True	False
5. Gina runs forty miles a week.	True	False
6. Emily wants to exercise at the gym.	True	False
7. Emily plans to start biking.	True	False

CONVERSATION

A ■◀ **Watch part of the video.**
Complete the conversation.

Gina: Want some fries?

Emily: _____, but I think I'd better pass. I've been gaining weight lately.

Gina: Really? It doesn't show at all.

Emily: Thanks, but I'm trying to cut down on the _____ and fat. And I have to limit the salt.

Gina: Oh, how come?

Emily: My doctor is concerned about my blood pressure. It's a bit high.

Gina: You've got _____ if you can stay away from these. I ought to be more careful, too. Since I get so much exercise I tend to think I can eat whatever I want.

> **Pronunciation Note**
>
> The word *to* usually has a short, weak pronunciation. In conversation, we often pronounce *have to* as "hafta" and *ought to* as "oughta."
>
> ◀)) **Listen and repeat.**
> I'm trying to cut down on fat.
> I have to ("hafta") limit the salt.
> I ought to ("oughta") be more careful.

B PAIRS **Practice the conversation.**

C PAIRS **Practice the conversation again. Make similar conversations. Talk about other eating and exercise habits.**

WHAT DO YOU THINK?

PAIRS Emily eats well but doesn't exercise. Gina exercises but doesn't eat well. What advice would you give Emily and Gina to help them change their habits?

GRAMMAR

Modals for advice

STUDY *should*, *ought to*, and *had better*

Statements

Emily **should** start exercising.
Gina **shouldn't** eat so much junk food.
I **ought to** make some changes in my diet.
He doesn't look well. He**'d better** go to the doctor.
I **had better not** eat fast food anymore.

Questions	Answers
Should I get a blood test?	Yes, you **should**.

Grammar Note
- *Had better* (*'d better*) is stronger than *should* and *ought to*.
- Don't use *ought to* in negative statements or questions.
- Use *should* in questions.

PRACTICE

A **Circle the correct words.**

To avoid diseases like high blood pressure and diabetes, you
(1) (should) / shouldn't eat a healthy diet. This can be difficult, but
you (2) had better / shouldn't focus on the foods you can't eat.
Instead, you (3) ought / should to think about the foods you
(4) should / had better not eat. Most importantly, you (5) ought to / shouldn't eat a lot
of fruit and vegetables. If you have signs of high blood pressure or high blood sugar, you
(6) had better / had better not make changes to your diet and start exercising right away.

B **Read about a typical day for Emily's supervisor, Sal. Then complete the advice
for him, using *should*, *shouldn't*, *ought to*, *had better*, or *had better not* and a verb.
More than one answer may be possible.**

Sal wakes up at 7:30 and rushes to work by 8:00. He has a cup of coffee,
but he doesn't eat breakfast. He usually gets a piece of pizza from the café for lunch.
When he feels tired in the afternoon, Sal gets a cup of coffee and a cookie.
Sal drives home and sits on the sofa to watch TV. He often falls asleep on the sofa.

Advice to Sal

1. You ___*should get up*___ earlier so you don't have to rush.
2. Breakfast is the most important meal of the day. You _____ a healthy breakfast.
3. You _____ fast food so often or you're going to get sick.
4. You _____ a piece of fruit from home instead of buying a cookie.
5. You _____ some exercise in the evening instead of sleeping in front of the TV.

WHAT ABOUT YOU?

PAIRS Imagine that you have some problems with your health. Work together to write a
list of six problems. (For example, *I'm tired a lot. I'm always sneezing.*) Meet with another pair
and share your lists. Give each other advice using *should*, *ought to*, and *had better*.

GET READY

Emily is concerned about her weight. She sits a lot and doesn't get much exercise. Do you or anyone you know sit a lot? Does it cause any health problems?

READ

◄))) **Listen and read the article. What is the main idea of the reading?**

Stand Up! Health Problems Related to Too Much Sitting

"Are you sitting down?" That's the question people ask when they're about to tell you something surprising. But I'm going to ask another question, "Are you standing up?"

If your answer is "no," then stand up before you read any further. Sitting too much causes a lot of health problems, such as weight gain or obesity, diabetes, and heart problems. For example, sitting too long slows the body's circulation. As a result, fewer calories burn and you gain weight. When you don't move, your body doesn't use as much blood sugar. The less blood sugar you use, the higher your risk of diabetes. Sitting also affects cholesterol levels, which can then lead to heart disease.

The advances in modern technology have led to more desk jobs, longer working hours, and a sedentary lifestyle. Things we used to do actively, we now do passively. We shop, pay bills, send mail, and work from our computers. When we're done, we entertain ourselves by playing video games, watching television, or going to the movies. We drive everywhere . . . even to nearby locations.

Some people think they're safe because they exercise. Even if you exercise the recommended 30 minutes a day, it's not enough to fight the hours we sit. The average person still sits seven and a half

hours at work, and that doesn't count time after work. We can't quit our jobs, so what can we do? We can fight the "sitting disease"!

There are some easy things you can do. Stand at your desk occasionally. Take the stairs. Let's go back to the mall rather than shopping online. Need to send an email to your boss? Don't. Walk to his or her office. Don't surf the Internet on your break. Take a walk around the building. Have a question for a colleague? Take a ten-minute walk to discuss it rather than calling or sending an email. You don't have to get rid of your television. Exercise or clean the house while you watch.

It's not too late! Join me! Stand up!

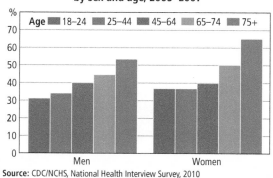

Inactive leisure-time behavior among adults by sex and age, 2005–2007

Age ■ 18–24 ■ 25–44 ■ 45–64 ■ 65–74 ■ 75+

Source: CDC/NCHS, National Health Interview Survey, 2010

Reading Skill

Writers have different reasons for writing. **Determining the author's purpose** helps you understand the writer's main ideas. There are three main purposes.

1. to inform: to give the reader facts and details
2. to persuade: to get the reader to agree with an opinion
3. to entertain: to get the reader to enjoy the writing

AFTER YOU READ

A Read the Reading Skill on page 64. Read the article again.
What do you think the author's purpose was? How do you know?

B Look at the graph. Read the statements. Circle *True* or *False*.
Correct the false statements.

1. In general, women are less active than men.	True	False
2. The most inactive age group is 45–64.	True	False
3. People get less active the older they get.	True	False
4. Men are least active when they are 25–44.	True	False
5. Women are most inactive when they are over 65.	True	False
6. Younger men are more active than older men.	True	False
7. Women between 18 and 24 are more active than men the same age.	True	False

VOCABULARY STUDY Collocations

Build Your Vocabulary

Collocations are words that are used together frequently.
For example:
weight gain
desk job
working hours
sedentary lifestyle
leisure time
surf the Internet

Read the Build Your Vocabulary note. Complete the sentences
with words from the list.

1. Modern technology, instead of saving time, usually leads to longer _____.

2. People who eat a lot of pizza and don't exercise may experience _____.

3. His _____ activities include golfing, jogging, and working on his car.

4. She's going to _____ to find websites about good vacation destinations.

5. Alfredo doesn't want a _____ in an office; he wants to be a construction
worker and be outside.

6. My grandmother has a _____. She doesn't exercise at all, and she
watches TV a lot.

WHAT DO YOU THINK?

PAIRS Discuss how you can change your daily habits to
be more active. Share your ideas with another pair.

ON THE WEB

For more information about this
topic, go online and search "avoid
sitting too much." Find one good tip
and report back to the class.

LISTENING AND SPEAKING

Plan an event

GET READY TO WATCH

Emily is the facilities manager in charge of the upcoming Business Department conference. Have you ever planned a large event or party? What did you have to do?

WATCH

◼◀ **Watch the video. Complete the sentences with the words from the box.**

> caterers   overtime   5:00   supervise   technology   umbrellas   8:00

1. Conference guests will begin arriving at _____ and will be gone by _____.
2. The _____ will set up breakfast and lunch.
3. There will be tables and _____ at the fountain plaza.
4. Emily thinks that the _____ will be ready in time for the conference.
5. Two security officers will be working _____ that day.
6. Emily is going to _____ the event.

CONVERSATION

Ⓐ ◼◀ **Watch part of the video. Complete the conversation.**

Sal: Emily! I've been meaning to ask you . . . How are things coming along for the Business Department _____?

Emily: I think we're all ready on our end.

Sal: Great! What's the schedule?

Emily: The guests will be arriving between 8:00 and 9:00 A.M., and the meetings will _____ from 9:00 to 4:00. They plan to have everyone out by 5:00.

Sal: How many people are coming?

Emily: Probably 250 to 300. Diana will have a more _____ number for me later this week.

> **Pronunciation Note**
>
> Some words have a syllable that is not usually pronounced.
>
> ◀))) **Listen and repeat.**
>
> business   conference
>
> everyone   everything

Ⓑ PAIRS **Practice the conversation. Use your own names.**

Ⓒ PAIRS **Practice the conversation again. Make similar conversations. Talk about a different future event, for example, a birthday party, a class party, or a student organization meeting.**

WHAT DO YOU THINK?

PAIRS Why do you think Emily is willing to come in on Saturday to supervise the event? Imagine you're Emily. Would you do the same thing? Why or why not?

Future continuous

STUDY Future Continuous

Sam **will be working** overtime that day.
I'll be studying until late tonight.
He **won't be eating** dinner with us because he has to leave.
Will you **be attending** the conference?
Who **will be setting up** the tables?

> **Grammar Note**
> - Future continuous describes an action that will continue over a period of time in the future.
> - You can also form the future continuous with *be going to + be* + a present participle. (*I'm going to be studying until late tonight.*)

PRACTICE

A Complete the sentences, using the future continuous with *will*.

1. After the conference, Emily ___will be preparing___ for
   prepare
   Family Day.

2. For this event, student organizations _____
   set up
   information tables.

3. On the day of the event, parents and family members _____ school.
   visit

4. They _____ information sessions about the college.
   attend

5. Emily is helping with preparations, but she _____ that Saturday.
   not work

B Read each answer. Write the question, using the word in parentheses and the future continuous with *will*.

1. **A:** _Where will the guests be sitting?_ _____ (Where)

   B: The guests will be sitting in the fountain plaza.

2. **A:** _____ (Who)

   B: The school administrators will be talking to the families.

3. **A:** _____ (What)

   B: They'll be talking about the college programs.

4. **A:** _____ (What time)

   B: The caterers will be serving lunch at 12:00.

5. **A:** _____ (What)

   B: They'll be serving chicken and salad.

WHAT ABOUT YOU?

GROUPS Take turns telling one another what you will be doing during the next few weeks. Do not repeat ideas. Continue until your teacher calls time. Share one thing you remember about your group members with the class.

Write a business letter

GET READY

Emily is planning an event for the PTA (parent-teacher association) at her sons' school. She writes a letter to a company to ask about their services. What do you think she will ask about?

STUDY THE MODEL

A Read the business letter. What information does Emily request?

615 Oak Road
Livingston, CA 91006

March 6, 2014

Tim Brothers Catering
522 Michaelson Drive
Crestwood, CA 90028

To Whom It May Concern:

I am the event organizer for the PTA at my sons' school. We are planning an orientation for parents whose children will be entering schools in the district in September. My boss suggested that I contact your company.

Your company has done catering for smaller events at other schools in the district. We were impressed with the quality of your food. This is our biggest event of the year. We are expecting 400 people to attend the event on May 10. I am currently looking for a catering company to supply food and drinks for breakfast, lunch, and one afternoon snack break.

I am writing to request your menu options and a price list for a large event such as the orientation. I'd also like to schedule a call to speak with your sales representative. I look forward to hearing from you.

Sincerely,

Emily Campos
Emily Campos

Writing Tip

Business letters follow a format and contain the same elements.

Your address	Body Paragraphs
Date	Closing
Recipient's Address	Signature
Greeting/Salutation	Name

B Read the Writing Tip. Read the business letter again.
Circle and label each part.

C Look at the chart Emily used to plan her writing and complete it.

Date	_____
Recipient's Address	Tim Brothers Catering 522 Michaelson Drive _____
Greeting	_____

Body	Planning orientation for _____
	Heard about you from _____
	Details about event:
	   Number of people _____
	   Date of event _____
	   Needs _____
	Requests:
	   menu options
	
	   _____
	   sales representative

Closing	_____

BEFORE YOU WRITE

You're going to write a business letter to a school or company requesting information. Plan your business letter on the chart.

Date	_____
Recipient's Address	_____ _____ _____
Greeting	_____
Body	Need information for _____ _____ Heard about you from _____ Details: _____ _____ Requests: _____ _____ _____
Closing	_____

WRITE

Review the Model and the Writing Tip on page 68. Use the ideas from your chart to write your business letter.

LESSON 7

PRACTICAL SKILLS

Read a medical history form

GET READY

Emily's friend Eva has an appointment with her doctor. Before she sees the doctor, she fills out a medical history form. Have you ever filled out a medical history form?

PRACTICAL READING

 Read Eva's completed medical history form. What is the purpose of a medical history form?

UNIVERSITY MEDICAL CENTER—PATIENT MEDICAL HISTORY

Name: _Eva Ortiz_   **Birth date:** _3/26/70_   **Date of visit:** _March 9, 2014_

Address: _1500 Sherman Drive, Long Beach, CA 90805_   **Phone #:** _714-555-5555_

Employer: _Sundale University_   **Social Security #:** _555-12-1234_

Medical insurance company: _Health Now Group Medical_   **Policy #:** _00-987-4343_

What is the reason for your visit today? _I would like to learn about safe and healthy ways to lose weight._

Check any of the following conditions that apply to you:

☐ Heart disease   ☐ Irregular heart beat   ☐ Diabetes
☐ Asthma   ☐ Kidney disease   ☐ Thyroid disease
☐ Stroke   ☐ Cancer or tumors   ☐ Lung disease / Tuberculosis
☐ Arthritis   ☐ Liver disease / Hepatitis   ☑ High or low blood pressure
☑ Smoking   ☑ Recent change in weight   ☐ Allergies

Explain here any conditions you checked. _I've had high blood pressure and have been taking medication for 3 months. I've gained about 20 pounds over the last year. I smoked from the age of 20 until 1 year ago._

	YES	NO
1. Is there a history of heart problems in your family?	☐	☑
2. Have you ever been hospitalized, had major operations, or had a serious illness?	☑	☐
If yes, explain. _I had thyroid problems as a child._		
3. Are you taking any drugs or medications now?	☑	☐
If yes, what? _Lisinopril for my high blood pressure_		
4. Are you allergic to any medications?	☐	☑
If yes, what?		
5. Are you on a special diet?	☐	☑
If yes, describe your diet.		
6. For women: Are you pregnant?	☐	☑

Patient Signature: _Eva Ortiz_   Date: _March 9, 2014_

B Read Eva's medical history form again. Circle the correct answers.

1. Why is Eva having an appointment with the doctor?
   a. She wants to quit smoking.
   b. She wants to lose weight.
   c. She wants to know about her own medical history.

2. Which of the statements is true about Eva?
   a. She's pregnant.
   b. She's still smoking.
   c. She's taking medications for high blood pressure.

3. Which of the statements is NOT true about Eva?
   a. She's allergic to Lisinopril.
   b. She doesn't have thyroid problems now.
   c. No one in her family has ever had heart problems.

C PAIRS Is it important to know your own medical history and the medical history of your family members? Why or why not?

PRACTICAL SPEAKING

A ◄))) The doctor is asking Eva about her medical history. Listen and read the conversation.

Dr. Taylor: Eva, tell me about your smoking. When you were smoking, how much did you smoke?

Eva: When I first started, I didn't smoke very much, but when I decided to quit, I was smoking more than one pack a day.

Dr. Taylor: And just to be sure, you're not smoking at all now?

Eva: I quit completely. I don't even like to smell cigarette smoke now.

B PAIRS Practice the conversation.

C PAIRS Look at Eva's medical history form again. Role play a similar conversation in which the doctor asks about other items on the form.

PRACTICAL LISTENING

◄))) Listen to a commercial for a new smartphone app. Read the statements. Circle *True* or *False*. Correct the false statements.

1. The "Track My BP" app takes your blood pressure.	True	False
2. The app reminds you to take your blood pressure medicine.	True	False
3. The app can display your blood pressure history as a chart.	True	False
4. The app allows you to send your blood pressure history to your doctor.	True	False
5. You have to enter the time and date for each blood pressure reading.	True	False
6. You have to download the app onto a computer before you can use it.	True	False

WHAT DO YOU THINK?

PAIRS Do you think apps such as "Track My BP" are useful? Do you think it's a good idea for people to track their own medical conditions? Why or why not?

GET READY TO WATCH

Emily is talking to Gina about stereotypes.
What are some common stereotypes that you have
heard or have seen in movies and on television?

WATCH

■◀ **Watch the video. Circle the correct answers.**

1. Gina's friend is hiring _____.
   a. an office helper
   b. a cell phone salesperson
   c. a computer technician

2. Gina thinks that the woman in her 60s is _____.
   a. a computer genius
   b. retired
   c. too old for the job

3. Gina finally agrees with Emily that _____.
   a. people in their 60s should retire
   b. the woman is probably good with computers
   c. personality is more important than age

4. Emily apologizes for _____.
   a. forgetting
   b. eavesdropping
   c. interrupting

 CONVERSATION

Ⓐ ■◀ **Watch part of the video. Complete part of the conversation.**

Emily: Gina, can I talk to you about something?

Gina: Yeah, sure. What is it?

Emily: I couldn't help _____ what you just said about older people.

Gina: Oh, yeah. A friend of mine is hiring some office help at his T-shirt company.
It really seems like a young person's job.

Emily: Don't you think you're kind of _____ older people, though?

Gina: Well, maybe, but 60s? That's like, retirement age.

Ⓑ **PAIRS Practice the conversation. Use your own names.**

Ⓒ **PAIRS Practice the conversation again. Make similar conversations.
Talk about the problem of stereotyping other groups of people.**

WHAT DO YOU THINK?

PAIRS Did Emily do the right thing by speaking to Gina about something she overheard?
Why or why not? Is it always important to speak out in these situations?
When is or isn't it important?

JOB-SEEKING SKILLS

Prepare a résumé

@RafikAramayan *Today*
Just updated my résumé!
It's posted on my job
page! Check it out!

GET READY

Rafik just updated his résumé. What kind of information should a résumé have?

PREPARE A RÉSUMÉ

A Read Rafik's résumé. What is his objective?

Rafik Aramayan
1000 Long Beach Blvd Apt. 320 • Long Beach, CA
562-555-5555 • rafik@rafikaramayan.com

Objective: Seeking a position in programming in which I can use my leadership, management, and problem-solving skills

Qualifications: • Skilled in finding quick and effective solutions to complicated technical problems
• Excellent as a team leader in software development group
• Proficient in computer programming languages such as Java, C++, and PHP

Experience: **1/2010 – 11/2013** Software Developer: Aerospace Systems. Team Leader for the Java/C++ Production Group. Managed budget of $12.4 million annually. Brought project in on schedule and under budget.

7/2009 – 12/2010 Programmer: Academic Devices. Assistant Database Programmer for School Information Systems Project. Analyzed client needs.

6/2008 – 7/2009 Assistant HTML Code Writer and Website Builder. Freelancer.

Education: Bachelor of Arts, Computer Science and Information Technology, 2009 Glendale University, Glendale, California

Awards: "Software Developer of the Month," Aerospace Systems, March 2012

References available upon request

B Read the statements. Circle *True* or *False*. Correct the false statements.

1. As a team leader at Aerospace Systems, Rafik managed a yearly budget of more than $12 million.   True   False
2. Rafik's most recent job was as a programmer at Academic Devices.   True   False
3. Rafik won the "Software Developer of the Month" award when he worked at Academic Devices.   True   False
4. Rafik has a BA in Computer Science and Information Technology.   True   False
5. Rafik doesn't have experience in website construction.   True   False

PUT YOUR IDEAS TO WORK

A Write your own résumé. Use Rafik's résumé as a model.

B PAIRS Show your résumé to your partner. Discuss who you will use as references. Why did you choose those people to be your references?

GRAMMAR

In this unit, you studied:
- *Should*, *ought to*, and *had better*
- Future continuous

See page 149 for your Grammar Review.

VOCABULARY See page 159 for the Unit 5 Vocabulary.

Vocabulary Learning Strategy: Make word webs

A Look at the words in the circles below. Make word webs with words from the list. For example:

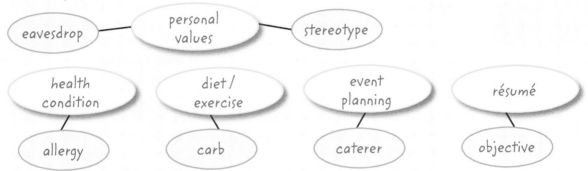

B Underline 5 words in Exercise A. Write a sentence with each word.

SPELLING See page 159 for the Unit 5 Vocabulary.

CLASS **Choose 10 words for a spelling test.**

LISTENING PLUS

A Watch each video. Write the story of Emily's day on a separate piece of paper.

Gina offers Emily some fries, but Emily says no. Emily thinks she's been gaining weight lately. She's trying to cut down on the carbs and fat.

B PAIRS **Review the conversation in Lesson 1** (see page 62).
Role play the conversation for the class.

NOW I CAN

PAIRS **See page 61 for the Unit 5 Goals.** Check ☑ the things you can do.
Underline the things you want to study more. Tell your partner.

I can _____. I need more practice with _____.

6

Diana Takes Charge

MY GOALS

☐ Complain about a bill

☐ Read a vehicle registration renewal notice

☐ Recall details about someone

☐ Take responsibility in a situation

☐ Write a cover letter

Go to MyEnglishLab for more practice after each lesson.

Diana Nhan

Diana　　　　　Today

I'm a problem solver. I like people to know they can rely on me.

Complain about a bill

GET READY TO WATCH

Diana is talking to the cable company about a problem with her bill. Have you ever had to call Customer Service about a problem with a bill? What happened?

WATCH

◼◀ **Watch the video. Answer the questions.**

1. What did the cable company charge Diana $15 for?

2. How long was the service offered for free?

3. Why is Diana not happy about the charge?

4. Why isn't the cable company going to send a new bill?

5. How much can Diana deduct from this month's bill?

CONVERSATION

A ◼◀ **Watch part of the video. Complete the conversation.**

Raymond: How can I help you today, Ms. Wu?

Diana: I was charged 15 extra dollars for something, and I don't understand why. It says "Zenith"?

Raymond: Oh, that's our new _____ movie channel. On Zenith you can see dozens of the newest releases every month.

Diana: I didn't order that.

Raymond: You were given a one-month free

_____ subscription.

Diana: But it's not free. You charged me $15.

Raymond: Yes, the one-month trial period ended in March.

Diana: And then it was added to my bill without my

_____?

B PAIRS **Practice the conversation. Use your own names.**

C PAIRS **Practice the conversation again. Make similar conversations. Talk about a service you were charged for but didn't order.**

> **Pronunciation Note**
>
> We stress the second syllable of numbers ending in -*teen* when we say the number by itself: thir**teen**. Stress often moves to the first syllable when another word follows: **thir**teen **days**. We always stress the first syllable of numbers ending in -*ty*: **thir**ty.
>
> ◀)) **Listen and repeat.**
>
> fif**teen**   **fif**teen **dol**lars
>
> **thir**ty   **thir**ty **days**

WHAT DO YOU THINK?

PAIRS The customer service representative offers to extend the free trial period. Why do you think Diana doesn't accept the offer? Do you think these kinds of offers are good or bad for consumers?

2 The passive voice

STUDY Present and Simple Past Passive

| A new tax **was added** to the bill. |
| Customer service calls **are** often **answered** by people in other countries. |
| We **weren't informed** about the changes to our account. |
| **Were** you **told** about the new services? |
| When **was** the cable **installed**? |

Grammar Note
- Use the passive to emphasize something that happened (or happens) rather than the person or thing (the *agent*) that caused it to happen.
- Use *by* with the passive to identify the agent.

PRACTICE

A Circle the correct verb forms.

1. The cable company (sent) / was sent a bill to Diana.
2. Diana charged / was charged more than she expected.
3. Her phone call answered / was answered by a man named Raymond.
4. Diana asked / was asked Raymond about the charges on her bill.
5. Raymond gave / was given Diana an explanation of the charges.
6. Diana's amount due adjusted / was adjusted.
7. The cable company didn't send / wasn't sent a new bill.

B Complete the paragraph with the verbs. Use the active or passive simple past.

A few years ago, Raymond thought phone calls to a cable company

_____were answered_____ by a cable company employee. Then he got the job at the call
 1. answer

center and _____ that wasn't true. Raymond _____
 2. discover   3. not employ

by the cable company at all. He _____ by a call center company.
 4. hire

The call center _____ Raymond to answer calls for High-Speed Cable
 5. train

Company. Other employees _____
 6. teach

how to answer calls for different cable or telephone

companies. A lot of people _____ to
 7. send

work in other countries, but Raymond works in the U.S.

WHAT ABOUT YOU?

PAIRS Write 6 complaints about a bill. Use the present and simple past passive. Share your sentences with a partner. Discuss whether you have the same problems and what to do about them.

> I'm charged a lot if I use my cell phone for too many minutes.

UNIT 6   77

Read a vehicle registration renewal notice

GET READY

Diana's sister Jill receives a notice in the mail notifying her that she has to renew the vehicle registration for her car. Have you ever renewed the registration of your car? What did you do?

PRACTICAL READING

A Read Jill's vehicle registration renewal notice from the Department of Motor Vehicles (DMV). What will happen if Jill doesn't renew her registration by April 2, 2014?

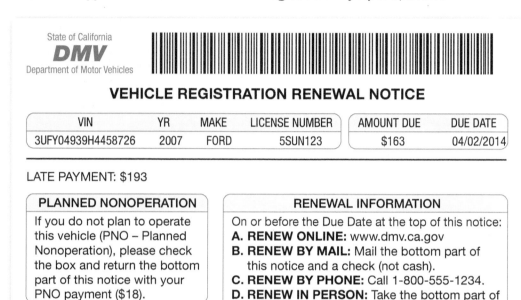

State of California
DMV
Department of Motor Vehicles

VEHICLE REGISTRATION RENEWAL NOTICE

VIN	YR	MAKE	LICENSE NUMBER		AMOUNT DUE	DUE DATE
3UFY04939H4458726	2007	FORD	5SUN123		$163	04/02/2014

LATE PAYMENT: $193

PLANNED NONOPERATION

If you do not plan to operate this vehicle (PNO – Planned Nonoperation), please check the box and return the bottom part of this notice with your PNO payment ($18).

RENEWAL INFORMATION

On or before the Due Date at the top of this notice:
A. **RENEW ONLINE:** www.dmv.ca.gov
B. **RENEW BY MAIL:** Mail the bottom part of this notice and a check (not cash).
C. **RENEW BY PHONE:** Call 1-800-555-1234.
D. **RENEW IN PERSON:** Take the bottom part of this notice to any DMV local office.

- - - - - - - - - - - **DETACH AND RETURN** - - - - - - - - - - -

License Number: 5SUN123
Make: Ford
VIN: 3UFY04939H445872
Due Date: 04/02/2014

Amount due if renewed on or before Due Date: $163
☐ Planned Nonoperation
☐ Change of Address (Fill out Change of Address Information on the back of this form.)

SEND PAYMENT TO:

DMV RENEWAL
P.O. BOX 942897
SACRAMENTO, CA 94297

B Read Jill's vehicle registration renewal notice again. Circle the correct answers.

1. How can Jill renew her registration?
   a. by mail　　　　**c.** online　　　**e.** all of the above
   b. by telephone　**d.** in person

2. How much will the total renewal fee for Jill's car be if she renews it online by April 2, 2014?
   a. $18　　　　**c.** $193
   b. $163　　　**d.** $163 plus $18 nonoperation fee

3. How much will the total renewal fee for her car be if she renews it by mail on April 3, 2014?
   a. $18　　　　**c.** $193
   b. $163　　　**d.** $163 plus $18 nonoperation fee

4. If Jill decides that she will not use her car at all, she must check the appropriate box on the form and return the bottom part of the form with a fee of _____.

    a. $18   **c.** $193

    b. $163   **d.** $163 plus $18 nonoperation fee

5. What must Jill do if she has moved since the last time she renewed her car registration?

    a. pay a fee of $18 to change her address

    b. return the form with her fee of $163 before the due date

    c. check the box on the front of the form, fill out the Change of Address information on the back of the form, and return the form with the appropriate fee

    d. renew her car registration as soon as possible

PRACTICAL SPEAKING

A ◀))) **Jill is talking on the phone with a DMV clerk about her registration renewal notice. Listen and read the conversation.**

Jill: I have a question about my registration renewal form.

Clerk: What would you like to know?

Jill: I'd like to pay with my credit card. Can I do that by mail?

Clerk: I'm sorry. If you're paying by mail, you can only use a check.

Jill: I see. When can I pay with my credit card?

Clerk: You can use your credit card when you pay online, over the phone, or in person at a DMV office.

Jill: OK. Thank you.

B PAIRS **Practice the conversation.**

C PAIRS **Look at the registration renewal notice again. Role play a similar conversation in which Jill asks the clerk other questions about the notice.**

PRACTICAL LISTENING

◀))) **Listen to the news program about vehicle registration renewal. Read the statements. Circle *True* or *False*. Correct the false statements.**

1. The Department of Motor Vehicles has increased the amount of time that car owners have to return their motor vehicle registration renewal fees.   True   False

2. If you return your motor vehicle registration renewal fee after the due date, you have to pay a late fee.   True   False

3. You can save money by returning your vehicle registration renewal form after the due date.   True   False

4. According to the news program, the penalties for a late vehicle registration renewal payment have increased.   True   False

WHAT DO YOU THINK?

PAIRS What are the advantages of renewing your registration online?
What can happen if you don't renew your vehicle registration at all?

GET READY TO WATCH

Diana's boss, Mark, can't remember someone he's met before. Does this happen to you often? What can we do to help us remember people?

WATCH

■◀ **Watch the video. Read the statements. Circle *True* or *False*. Correct the false statements.**

1.	Dr. Jain is tall and thin.	True	False
2.	Mark spoke to Dr. Jain for 20 minutes.	True	False
3.	Dr. Jain recommended a Japanese restaurant to Mark.	True	False
4.	Diana remembers the name of the restaurant.	True	False
5.	Dr. Jain's first name is Anish.	True	False

CONVERSATION

 ■◀ **Watch part of the video. Complete the conversation.**

Mark: Who is Dr. Jain?

Diana: He's the _____ professor from Stanton.

Mark: Do I know him?

Diana: You met him at the pre-conference _____.

Mark: Is he the tall, thin guy who ate all those shrimp?

Diana: No. He's short and _____.

Mark: Oh, OK. Is he the one who showed me a picture of his new girlfriend?

Diana: No, that wasn't him either. He's married, and I'm pretty sure he has three or four children.

 PAIRS **Practice the conversation.**

 PAIRS **Practice the conversation again. Make similar conversations. Pretend that you can't remember a current classmate. Your partner describes the person to help you remember. Then change roles.**

WHAT DO YOU THINK?

PAIRS Imagine Mark receives a call from Dr. Jain and has no idea who he is. What should Mark do? Should he pretend to remember Dr. Jain, or should he be honest? Why?

GRAMMAR

Adjective clauses

STUDY Adjective Clauses

Relative Pronouns as Subject
I picked up the papers **that fell off the desk**.
Is that the man **who came to the party**?
The woman **that works in the Dean's Office** is very nice.

Relative Pronouns as Object
The book **(that) he wrote** is very interesting.
The woman **(who) we saw at the reception** is here.
Where is the professor **(that) you introduced me to** last year?

Grammar Note

- Use *who* or *that* to introduce adjective clauses about people. Use *that* to introduce adjective clauses about things.
- We often omit object relative pronouns, especially in speaking.

PRACTICE

A Complete the paragraph with *who*, *that*, or Ø. Use Ø if the relative pronoun can be omitted.

Administrative assistants are people (1) _who (that)_ work in an office helping a manager. They often solve problems (2) _____ the manager doesn't have time for. The job duties (3) _____ they have can vary. They usually deal with any correspondence (4) _____ comes in for the manager. They're usually the ones (5) _____ answer the phone for the manager, too.

B On a separate piece of paper, combine the underlined pairs of sentences into one. Make the second sentence an adjective clause.

Do you have trouble remembering people's names? <u>Here are tips. They can help you remember names.</u> Repeat the names. <u>People tell you the names.</u> Asking people to spell their names for you will also help. <u>Now imagine you see a man. You have met him before.</u> You can't remember his name. Try introducing yourself first. He'll probably tell you his name, too. <u>In a formal situation, people may have business cards. The business cards will tell you the name.</u> When you say goodbye, ask the person for a card.

> *Here are tips that can help you remember names.*

WHAT ABOUT YOU?

PAIRS Write 8 "mystery sentences" about familiar people and things. Use 4 relative pronouns as subjects and 4 relative pronouns as objects. Meet with another pair and see if they can guess the answers.

> *This is the holiday that falls on a Monday in May.*
> *This is the politician everyone was talking about last week.*

6

Scan for specific information

GET READY

Diana calls customer service about an unexpected charge on her cable bill. Have you ever had an unexpected charge? What happened?

READ

◀))) **Listen and read the article. What do all these people have in common?**

Call Them on That!

Lili Lu was shocked when her phone bill arrived; it was $24 more than usual. The worst part was, she didn't know why. "I hadn't called anyone, not even my mother in China." Raj Singh had a similar experience. His phone bill was $28 more. "It was tricky," he said, "I trusted the company. I paid the fees for three months before I complained."

Lili and Raj were crammed, and they're not alone. The Federal Communications Commission (FCC) estimates that 15 to 20 million U.S. households are victims every year. Cramming is when companies put extra charges on your bill. Those charges are not approved and are confusing because they look legitimate. In fact, only 1 out of every 20 victims may notice, which shows you how real the charges look.

Ana Gomez agreed that it was misleading. "When you see the words 'service charge' or 'calling plan' you don't really think about it." Those sound "normal." Raj also noted that the charges were tiny. "Two dollars here or three dollars there. I didn't really notice." Companies do that deliberately because small charges are less noticeable, but they add up.

Lili warns everyone to look carefully. "I keep a list of my calls now. It's like homework! If I don't do my homework, I'm going to lose when my bill comes. If I don't know what the charge is for, I want it removed. I need my money more than the phone company needs it." Lili also suggests reading carefully before signing up for any new services. The fine print is important. Ana agrees. "Sometimes those charges are hidden in that small writing!"

These victims offer some advice. Think before you sign up for trial offers on the Internet. People forget to cancel the trial and get charged for the service the next month. Lili said, "I didn't even sign up for the service. The free coupon service was a 'gift.' I didn't know the gift was for only a month. I wanted to save money by downloading grocery coupons. I saved a few measly cents with the coupons, but it cost a lot more on my phone bill!" Raj, Lili, and Ana agree you should not be afraid to call the company or complain to the FCC. The charges start small, but they cost a lot over time. Raj said, "Don't get crammed. Call them on it!"

Reading Skill

Scanning is looking at a reading quickly to find specific information. Move your eyes across the page, focusing only on specific information such as names, numbers, dates, or key words.

AFTER YOU READ

Read the Reading Skill on page 82. Scan the article and answer the questions.

1. Lili's bill was larger than usual. How much extra was she charged?

2. How many households are victims every year?

3. How many victims are aware of the cramming charges?

4. What is an example of what a cramming charge is called on a bill?

5. Who should you call to file a complaint?

VOCABULARY STUDY Context Clues

> **Build Your Vocabulary**
>
> Sometimes you can figure out the meaning of a word from **context clues—** the words before or after it. For example:
>
> *Raj Singh also noted that the charges were tiny. "Two dollars here or three dollars there. I didn't really notice."*
>
> If you read the sentence after the word, you can figure out that *tiny* means *small*.

Read the Build Your Vocabulary note. Then guess what these words mean from the context.

1. The fine print is important. Ana agreed. "Sometimes those charges are hidden in that small writing!"

fine print = _____

2. Those charges are not approved and are confusing because they look legitimate. In fact, only 1 out of every 20 victims may notice, which shows you how real the charges look.

legitimate = _____

3. Ana Gomez agreed that it was misleading. "When you see the words 'service charge' or 'calling plan' you don't really think about it."

misleading = _____

4. I wanted to save money by downloading grocery coupons. I saved a few measly cents with the coupons, but it cost a lot more on my phone bill!

measly = _____

WHAT DO YOU THINK?

PAIRS Do you think it's fair to ask consumers to call the company to cancel a free trial service? Imagine one of you works for a phone company and the other is a consumer. Express your opinions. Share your opinions with the class.

> **ON THE WEB**
>
> For more information about this topic, go online and search "phone cramming." Report back to the class.

GET READY

Diana needs to write instructions for a fire emergency. What kind of information do you expect to find in emergency instructions?

STUDY THE MODEL

A **Read the instruction memo. What is the first step in dealing with a fire emergency?**

MEMO

To: All Staff
From: Diana Nhan, Administrative Assistant
Subject: In Case of Fire

Although we hope that we will not have a fire, we want to take a moment to remind everyone of the official procedure to follow.

First, if possible, determine what is on fire and where the fire is located. This is useful information to have for emergency services, but do not put yourself in danger to find the fire. Then call 911 to report the fire. Be prepared to tell them your name, location, and any details you know about the fire.

If the fire is already too big, leave the building immediately! You can call 911 after you exit the building. For those of you on the second and third floors, do not use the elevator. Everyone needs to use the stairs to get to the first floor and the exits. Remember to avoid smoke by crawling. This will keep you from breathing in smoke.

Do not open doors without first checking to see if the door is hot. If the door is hot when you touch it, do not open it. There is likely fire on the other side. Try and find another way to leave the building.

Take a few minutes this week to plan an escape route from your office to the nearest exit. Plan an extra escape route in case your first route is blocked. The entire procedure should take less than five minutes. We want all of our employees to be safe at work.

Writing Tip

It is important to think about your **audience** when you are writing. Think about who is in your audience, what they need, and the most important things for them to know.

B **Read the Writing Tip. Read the memo again. Underline words and phrases that indicate the specific audience.**

C. Look at the instructional guidelines that Diana used to plan the memo and complete it.

What to do in case of fire

Specific audience: _____

Resources: phone _____

Estimated time: _____

Details:

Determine information about the fire (if possible).

_____

Be prepared to tell them your name, location, and details.

Leave the building.

Do not use the _____.

Use the _____.

Crawl.

Check the doors. Do not open if they are too hot.

Plan a route from office to exit.

_____

BEFORE YOU WRITE

You're going to write an emergency plan for your workplace, school, or home. Use the instructional guideline to plan your writing.

What to do in case of _____

Specific audience: _____

Resources: _____

Estimated time: _____

Details:

_____

_____

_____

_____

_____

_____

_____

_____

_____

WRITE

Review the Model and the Writing Tip. Use the ideas from your instructional guideline to write your emergency plan.

GET READY TO WATCH

The student is frightened about an unusual animal she just saw. Have you ever seen any unusual animals at your home or school? What happened?

WATCH

 Watch the video. Read the statements. Circle *True* **or** *False.* **Correct the false statements.**

1.	When the student saw the animal, she slammed the door shut.	True	False
2.	The student knows what the animal is.	True	False
3.	The student was hurt.	True	False
4.	Diana asks Paula to lock the door.	True	False
5.	Diana calls Animal Control first.	True	False
6.	The animal removal service will arrive in about two hours.	True	False

CONVERSATION

A   **Watch part of the video. Complete the conversation.**

Student: There's an animal in the bathroom!

Diana: An animal? What kind of animal?

Student: I don't know. It's about the size of a cat, but it's not a cat. I didn't see it very closely.

I _____ the door shut as soon as I saw it.

Diana: It's probably an opossum. We have a lot of them around here. Which bathroom?

Student: The women's room down the hall, on the first floor.

Diana: OK. I'm going to _____ the door.

B PAIRS **Practice the conversation.**

C PAIRS **Practice the conversation again. Make similar conversations. Report a potentially dangerous situation. Explain what you are going to do about it.**

Pronunciation Note

When a word begins with a vowel sound, we usually link it to the word that comes before it.

◀)) **Listen and repeat. Do not stop your voice between the linked words.**

There's an animal in the bathroom!

It's about the size of a cat.

I didn't see it.

WHAT DO YOU THINK?

PAIRS Diana takes responsibility in a potentially dangerous situation. How about Paula and the student? Do they do everything they should? What, if anything, would you do differently?

@RafikAramayan *Today*
I've been writing cover letters all day! I posted one on my job page. Read it and decide: "Would you hire me?"

GET READY

Rafik writes a cover letter for every résumé that he sends to a company. What is the purpose of a cover letter?

WRITE A COVER LETTER

Read Rafik's cover letter. Read the statements. Circle *True* or *False*. Correct the false statements.

Rafik Aramayan
1000 Long Beach Blvd., Apt. 320   Long Beach, CA 90801
562-555-5555   rafik@rafikaramayan.com — **Contact information**

March 12, 2014

CloseFit
2734 San Rafael Way   San Francisco, CA 94134 — **Employer contact information**

Dear Human Resources Manager: — **Salutation**

I am applying for the Software Developer position. At your convenience, I'd appreciate the opportunity to discuss the position and my suitability for this position with you. You can find my résumé attached to this letter. — **Why you are writing**

I have experience in multiple programming languages and have served as the Team Leader for a software development group. I have created multiple websites and have demonstrated leadership, goal-setting, and problem-solving experience. I believe that my strong technical experience and education will make me a very competitive candidate for this position. — **What you have to offer; why you will be good for the company**

I would welcome the opportunity to tell you how my skills can benefit CloseFit. Thank you for your consideration. I look forward to hearing from you soon! — **Asking for an interview and thanking the person**

> **Body**

Sincerely, — **Closing**

Rafik Aramayan — **Signature**
Rafik Aramayan

---

1. Rafik lists his address, telephone number, and email address in the contact information section of the cover letter.   True   False

2. You describe why you think it will be beneficial for the company to hire you in the salutation.   True   False

3. In the first paragraph of the body of a cover letter, it is important to explain why you are writing.   True   False

4. *Sincerely* is a common salutation in a cover letter.   True   False

PUT YOUR IDEAS TO WORK

PAIRS Pick one of the job ads in Unit 3. Write a cover letter to the company. Use Rafik's letter as a guide. Read your partner's cover letter. Do you think the cover letter will make the human resources manager invite your partner for an interview? Why or why not?

GRAMMAR

In this unit, you studied:

- Present and simple past passive
- Adjective clauses

See page 150 for your Grammar Review.

VOCABULARY See page 159 for the Unit 6 Vocabulary.

Vocabulary Learning Strategy: Learn words from different meanings in different contexts

A Choose at least 3 words from the list. Write down 2 meanings for each word. Use a dictionary. For example:

make	1.	_do or produce something_
	2.	_a particular type of product, made by one company_
_____	1.	_____
	2.	_____
_____	1.	_____
	2.	_____
_____	1.	_____
	2.	_____

B Circle 5 meanings in Exercise A. Write a sentence for each meaning.

SPELLING See page 159 for the Unit 6 Vocabulary.

CLASS Choose 10 words for a spelling test.

LISTENING PLUS

A Watch each video. Write the story of Diana's day on a separate piece of paper.

> _Diana is speaking to a customer service representative about a problem with her cable bill. She was charged extra fees for something she didn't order._

B **PAIRS** Review the conversation in Lesson 8. (See page 86.) Role play the conversation for the class.

NOW I CAN

PAIRS **See page 75 for the Unit 6 Goals.** Check ☑ the things you can do. Underline the things you want to study more. Tell your partner.

> I can _____. I need more practice with _____.

7 Ben Makes a Difference

MY GOALS

- ☐ Talk about volunteer work
- ☐ Deal with workplace gossip
- ☐ Read a credit card application
- ☐ Talk about financial responsibility
- ☐ Prepare for a job interview

Go to MyEnglishLab for more practice after each lesson.

Ben Ramírez

Ben   *Today*
I believe we can make a difference in other people's lives if we choose to.

LISTENING AND SPEAKING

1 Talk about volunteer work

GET READY TO WATCH

Amaya wants Ben to volunteer at a school event.
Have you ever done volunteer work?
What did you do?

WATCH

■◀ **Watch the video. Read the statements. Circle** *True* **or** *False.*
Correct the false statements.

1. Ben is surprised to see Amaya.	True	False
2. Amaya has been preparing for Family Day.	True	False
3. A few student groups are participating in Family Day.	True	False
4. As a volunteer, Ben will help the teachers on Family Day.	True	False
5. Ben is going to volunteer for three hours.	True	False

CONVERSATION

A ■◀ **Watch part of the video. Complete the conversation.**

Amaya: You know, we can always use a few more staff volunteers.

Ben: What would I have to do?

Amaya: Nothing difficult. We just need people to staff the tables at the front entrance.

Ben: I suppose I could do that.

Amaya: You hand _____ to parents. You give them directions to places on campus, answer questions, that kind of thing.

Ben: OK. It's this Saturday, right?

Amaya: Yep. We'd like volunteers to be here around 3:00. You'll be finished by 6:00.

Ben: I can _____ that.

> **Pronunciation Note**
>
> The vowel in a stressed syllable has a long, clear sound. The vowels in unstressed syllables often have the very short, unclear sound /ə/.
>
> ◀)) **Listen and repeat.**
>
> párents   cámpus   suppóse
>
> banána   promótion   voluntéers

B PAIRS **Practice the conversation.**

C PAIRS **Practice the conversation again. Make similar conversations. Volunteer for a job in the classroom or on campus.**

WHAT DO YOU THINK?

PAIRS Why do you think Ben agrees to volunteer for a school event on Saturday?
It is not unusual for schools and universities to ask employees to volunteer time or to attend special occasions out of their regular hours. Do you think this is acceptable? Why or why not?

Placement of direct and indirect objects

 STUDY **Direct and Indirect Objects**

Verb + Indirect Object + Direct Object	Verb + Direct Object + Preposition + Indirect Object
He brought **his girlfriend** a sandwich.	He brought a sandwich to **his girlfriend**.
She's going to buy **him** presents.	She's going to buy presents for **him**.
Ben showed **his friend** the picture.	Ben showed the picture to **his friend**.
	He brought it to **his girlfriend**. NOT He brought ~~his girlfriend it.~~

Grammar Note

When the direct object is a pronoun, always use this order:
verb + direct object pronoun + preposition + indirect object.

 PRACTICE

A **Put the words in the correct order to make sentences.**

1. his friend / a muffin / brought / Ben / for _Ben brought a muffin for his friend._

2. it / Amaya / to / explained / her coworker _____

3. will give / directions / them / Ben _____

4. wants to / he / dinner / her / buy _____

5. handed / the woman / he / it / to _____

6. the pictures / showed / Ben / them _____

B **On a separate piece of paper, rewrite the sentences, switching the order of the direct and indirect objects if possible. Some sentences cannot be re-ordered.**

1. She bought books for them. _She bought them books._

2. Amaya showed the program to him.

3. She sent him an email.

4. He bought it for her.

5. The student brought her the information.

6. The caterers served refreshments to them.

7. He lent it to him last year.

WHAT ABOUT YOU?

GROUP **Student A:** Say a sentence with one of these verbs: *bring, give, hand, lend, offer, pass, read, sell, send, serve, show.* Use a direct and indirect object.
Student B: Restate your partner's sentence, changing the placement of the indirect object. Then choose a different verb and say a new sentence. Continue taking turns around the group.

He gave me a book.   He gave a book to me.

3 Identify cause and effect

GET READY

Ben volunteers to help Amaya at Family Day. Do you volunteer?
Why do you think people volunteer?

READ

◀))) **Listen and read the article. How did the person start volunteering?**

Why I Volunteer: An Interview with Venice Town's Volunteer of the Year Winner
— by Eliana Gomez

I had the opportunity to talk with Nadine Schmidt, winner of this year's Volunteer of the Year award in Venice Town. I asked Nadine about her service and her motivations.

EG: Congratulations! Were you surprised you won?

NS: Oh, yes. I had no idea the award existed.

EG: Why do you volunteer then?

NS: There are some specific reasons. I started volunteering when I was 16 because, at that time, it was required by my school. We earned academic credit.

EG: What was your first service?

NS: My memory is a little foggy, but I'm sure it was when I volunteered at the hospital. I ran errands for nurses, held babies, and delivered mail to patients. After I finished my credit, I kept going since I realized I loved being there for the patients. Some of them didn't have many visitors and they were lonely. I think it made them feel good and I felt good, too, even though I was dead some nights!

EG: What did you do next?

NS: The next job I did was tutoring children at the elementary school. I wanted to be a teacher. Therefore, volunteering was a chance to see if I would really like that career.

EG: Did you like it?

NS: I loved it. Kids were the apple of my eye; I adored them. After I got my degree in education, I moved to Venice Town. At the beginning, I didn't know anyone. I felt so isolated. My home was a prison! I needed to do something. I did a little research and discovered Venice Town's Food Bank needed volunteers to help

distribute food to the homeless. I started working there once a week, and consequently I made friends with a lot of the other volunteers. We're still friends today! They are my rocks in hard times.

EG: Do you do any other volunteering?

NS: I also volunteer at Dress Up! This organization collects clothing for women who are unemployed and trying to get back on their feet. We clean and repair donated business suits for the women to wear to job interviews, thus helping them succeed. It's fun helping women pick out clothes and watching them get a better life.

EG: Wow. Do you have any time for yourself?

NS: I could if I wanted to. But this keeps me busy, and I don't like to be bored.

EG: Well, congratulations on the award. I can see why you were the winner.

AFTER YOU READ

A **Read the Reading Skill. Read the article again. Underline the cause-and-effect words.**

> **Reading Skill**
>
> Writers sometimes write about the reasons they do something (the causes) and the results (the effects). **Identifying cause and effect** helps you understand why the subject did something. Here are some key words that help identify cause and effect.
>
> | | |
> |---|---|
> | because | if/then |
> | since | so |
> | therefore | as a result |
> | consequently | due to |
> | thus | in order to |

B **Match the causes and effects.**

_____ **1.** Nadine started volunteering

_____ **2.** Nadine loved being there for the patients;

_____ **3.** Since Nadine wanted to be a teacher,

_____ **4.** Nadine felt she needed to do something;

_____ **5.** Nadine helps repair clothes for women,

a. consequently, she volunteered at the Food Bank.

b. therefore, she kept visiting the hospital.

c. thus helping those women succeed.

d. because it was required by school.

e. she decided to be a tutor first.

VOCABULARY STUDY Metaphors

> **Build Your Vocabulary**
>
> A **metaphor** is a way of describing something by comparing it to something that has similar qualities, without using _like_ or _as_. For example:
> _Our company gave us the green light to dress casually on Fridays._
> (give someone the green light = allow someone to do something)

Read the Build Your Vocabulary note. Then match the metaphors and definitions.

_____ **1.** foggy

_____ **2.** dead

_____ **3.** apple of my eye

_____ **4.** a prison

_____ **5.** a rock

a. a place where you feel trapped and can't escape

b. not as clear as it could be

c. something that makes you feel strong

d. something you like or cherish

e. very tired

WHAT DO YOU THINK?

PAIRS What kind of volunteering do you do or do you want to do? Why?

> **ON THE WEB**
>
> For more information about this topic, go online and search "volunteer opportunities" and the name of your city. Report back to the class.

GET READY TO WATCH

Rochelle is talking about Ben's supervisor. Do you know people who often say negative things about others? How do you respond to them?

WATCH

 Watch the video. Answer the questions.

1. Why does Rochelle think Karen is in trouble?
2. What happened between Karen and Dean Winters?
3. Why doesn't Ben pay attention to Karen's schedule?
4. What was Professor Clifford doing?
5. Why doesn't Ben want to hear about Karen's problems?
6. What does Rochelle say about Arnold?

CONVERSATION

A **Watch part of the video. Complete the conversation.**

Rochelle: You know, Karen isn't at the administrators' meeting. I think she may be in trouble.

Ben: Because she's not at the meeting? That seems like a stretch. She might have other things to do.

Rochelle: Well, she got into an _____ with Dean Winters yesterday.

Ben: I don't know anything about that. So what?

Rochelle: When he walked by the office this morning, he looked _____. He must still be upset with her.

Ben: Come on, Rochelle. He could be upset about something else altogether.

Rochelle: Like what?

Ben: Maybe he was thinking about last night's game or about politics. Or he might not be upset at all. Maybe he has _____ .

B PAIRS **Practice the conversation. Use your own names.**

C PAIRS **Practice the conversation again. Make similar conversations. Suggest possible reasons why one of your classmates is not in class today.**

WHAT DO YOU THINK?

PAIRS Why doesn't Ben want to get involved in this conversation with Rochelle? What effect does gossip have on a workplace?

Modals of possibility and conclusion

○○○○○§○
STUDY Modals of Possibility and Conclusion

They **may** have a problem.	She **may not** know how to solve the problem.
Karen **might** want to talk to the dean.	The dean **might not** want to talk to Karen.
She **could** be at a different meeting.	It **couldn't** be a very important meeting.
Arnold **must** work with Ben and Rochelle.	Karen **must not** be happy about the gossip.
	She **can't** be at lunch. It's too early.

> **Grammar Note**
>
> *Maybe* has the same meaning as *could*, *might*, and *may*, but it is
> not a modal. (**Maybe** *it's something personal.*)

PRACTICE

A **Circle the correct modals.**

1. Ben and Rochelle have worked together for three years. They (might)/ can't be friends.

2. Ben got four hours of sleep last night. He must / might not be tired.

3. Karen knows Rochelle was talking about her. She couldn't / may be annoyed.

4. Ben is trying to ignore Rochelle. He must / must not want to hear the gossip.

5. Rochelle spends a lot of time at work chatting. She could / must not be very busy.

6. I saw Ben playing tennis this morning. He must / can't be out sick today.

B **Read the conversations. Rewrite the underlined sentences.**
Use the words in parentheses.

1. **A:** Can you hear them yelling in the meeting?

   B: Yes, I can! I think they're angry. (must)
   They must be angry.

2. **A:** The secretary isn't answering the phone.

   B: She's probably at lunch. (might)

   _____

3. **A:** Look at Karen. She's frowning at her email.

   B: I'm pretty sure she doesn't like what it says. (must not) _____

4. **A:** Rochelle is already back from the meeting.

   B: That's impossible! I don't believe she's back already! (can't) _____

5. **A:** Did you see that guy who looks like Ben?

   B: Maybe he's Ben's brother. (could) _____

WHAT ABOUT YOU?

PAIRS Write 4 situations. Then meet with another pair.
Take turns drawing conclusions about each other's situations.

A very large package is delivered to our classroom. Our teacher can't lift it.

It must be heavy. It might be a new desk.

GET READY

Ben receives a thank-you note for volunteering at Family Day.
When do people send out thank-you notes?

STUDY THE MODEL

 Read the thank-you note that Ben received. Why did the writer send the note?

April 15, 2014

Dear Ben,

I am writing to thank you for volunteering at Family Day last Saturday. Having your help at the Welcome table made the registration process run smoothly and efficiently. I appreciate your giving up personal time to work at the university.

Family Day was a huge success. Over 300 families visited campus for tours, seminars, and activities after an opening address by the university president. Family members had the opportunity to attend the football game, shop at the bookstore, and visit other campus facilities.

Thanks to volunteers like you, the university was able to impress new families, welcome back alumni, and show why it is one of the best universities in the region. I couldn't have done it without you.

Thanks again,

William Michaels

William Michaels

Family Day Coordinator

Writing Tip

Writers have a **purpose** for writing. The purpose should be clearly stated and explained.

 Read the Writing Tip. Read the note again. Underline the writer's purpose for writing. Where did you find it?

C **Look at and complete the chart the writer used to plan his writing.**

Recipient: Ben	Purpose: say "thank you" for volunteering

Event:	Where / When:

Specific details: welcome table, helped with registration process

Event details:
300 families
visited campus for _____
_____

address by president
attended football game

university impressed _____
welcomed back alumni
showed university as one of the best in the region

Closing: Thanks again.

 BEFORE YOU WRITE

You're going to write a thank-you note for a dinner party you've just attended.
Use the chart below to plan your note.

Recipient:	Purpose:

Event:	Where / When:

Specific details:

Event details:

Closing:

 WRITE

Review the Model and the Writing Tip. Use the ideas from your chart
to write your thank-you note.

GET READY

Ben's brother Abe receives an offer to get a new credit card in the mail. He fills out the credit card application and mails it back. Have you ever filled out a credit card application?

PRACTICAL READING

  Read Abe's credit card application. What can happen if Abe doesn't make a payment by the due date on his credit card billing statement?

American Bank of Long Beach: Credit Card Application Form

Cardholder Information			
Name (Last, First, Middle) Ramírez, Abe		Name to appear on Card (20 letter maximum) Abe Ramírez	
Birth date (MM/DD/YYYY) 05/20/1988	Place of Birth Whittier, CA	Mother's Maiden Name González	Social Security Number 555-12-1234
Home Address (Street No., Street, Apartment No., City, State) 3438 Beachfront Way, Apt 201 Long Beach, CA			Zip Code 90805

Home Phone 424-555-1234	Do you own a home? Yes ____ No ✓	Do you own a car? Yes ✓ No ____	Education ✓ High School
Cell Phone 424-555-5555	Mortgage payment? Yes ____ No ✓ Renting?	Financed? Yes ✓ No ____	✓ College Graduate ___ Postgraduate ___ Doctorate
Email Address Abe_ramirez@hwn.com	Yes ✓ No ____ Other _____		

Cardholder's Work and Financial Information			
Employer's Name Project Inc.		Position Sales Coordinator	
Address (Street No., Street, Suite No., City, State, Zip) 100 Penn Blvd., Long Beach, CA 90805		Work Phone 714-555-5555	Years/Months at this job 4 years 2 months
Gross Annual Income ($) 55,000	Other Income ($) 6,000	Sources of Other Income Home-based Internet Sales Business	

Bank Accounts		
Bank Name CaliBank	Type of Account Checking	Account Number 89-97634211
Bank Name CaliBank	Type of Account Savings	Account Number 89-97634200

Disclosures		
Summary of Account Terms		
Annual Percentage Rate for Purchases	7.24% to 21.24% variable; default APR 31.74%	
Cash Advance APR	22.99% variable	
Your annual percentage rate may vary monthly.	Your annual percentage rate may vary monthly.	
Grace Period	20–25 days for purchases only	
Annual Membership Fee	$24.00	
Cash Advance Fee	4.00% of the transaction amount. $10.00 minimum	
Late Payment Fee	Balance up to $200.00	$27.00
	Balance of $201.00 and more	$39.00

B Look at Abe's credit card application again. Read the statements. Circle *True* or *False*. Correct the false statements.

1. The last name of Abe's mother before she got married was González.   True   False

2. Abe's only income is from his job at Project Inc.   True   False

3. The annual percentage rate on this credit card will never change.   True   False

4. Abe will have to pay a fee of $24 to keep his card each year.   True   False

5. If Abe has a balance of $500 on his credit card, and his payment is late, the bank will charge him a $27 fee.   True   False

PRACTICAL SPEAKING

A ◄))) Abe is asking a bank clerk questions about the credit card application. Listen and read the conversation.

Abe: Could you tell me what "default APR" means?

Clerk: Sure. The "default APR" is the usual "annual percentage rate" for this type of credit card.

Abe: That's 31.74%. It's very high.

Clerk: When you start a new account, the APR is lower. But if your monthly payment is late, the bank will raise your monthly APR to the higher "default" rate.

B PAIRS Practice the conversation.

C PAIRS Look at the credit card application again. Role play a similar conversation in which Abe asks the clerk other questions about the application.

PRACTICAL LISTENING

◄))) Listen to the public service announcement from the Federal Trade Commission. Circle the correct answers.

1. How can criminals steal your money without actually having your card?
   a. by finding your card number on a discarded receipt
   b. by adding amounts to blank spaces on a receipt
   c. by getting your account information by offering a fake "trip" via a mailing
   d. all of the above

2. When should you report a lost or stolen credit card?
   a. 24 hours after you learn that it was lost or stolen
   b. immediately
   c. after you've found it
   d. after you've reported the loss or theft to the police

3. What is one way to prevent credit card fraud?
   a. always compare your receipts to your bills
   b. lend your card to others
   c. join bargain travel clubs that you learn about from mailings
   d. give your account number to people who call you

WHAT DO YOU THINK?

PAIRS Compare your own experiences with credit cards. What are the positive and negative aspects of having credit cards?

LISTENING AND SPEAKING

Talk about financial responsibility

GET READY TO WATCH

Ben's brother, Abe, doesn't pay off his credit card bills. Do you pay off your credit card bills? Why or why not?

WATCH

■◀ **Watch the video. Circle the correct answers.**

1. Abe got a Premiere card because _____.
   a. he has a lot of debt
   b. they offered him a good deal
   c. he had a balance on another card

2. Abe is carrying credit card debt because _____.
   a. he had to make large purchases quickly
   b. he doesn't like to spend cash
   c. it's a good deal

3. Ben thinks that credit card companies _____.
   a. lure people in with offers   b. offer good deals   c. help people make a fortune

CONVERSATION

A ■◀ **Watch part of the video. Complete the conversation.**

Ben: Abe, why are you carrying balances on your credit cards?

That's such a _____ of money.

Abe: I just had a lot of expenses this year, you know, but I've got it under control.

Ben: OK, if you say so.

Abe: It's just for a few months. I had to make a couple of big purchases all of a sudden.

And I've got good _____!

Ben: Oh yeah?

Abe: Yes. I'm being promoted to assistant manager in a couple of months.

Ben: Congratulations! That's great. That should help you get out of _____.

Pronunciation Note

The words *of* and *for* usually have a short, weak pronunciation with the vowel sound /ə/. We link these words to the words around them.

◀))) **Listen and repeat. Notice that *of* can sound like the word *a* before a consonant sound.**

That's such a waste of money.

I had a lot of expenses.

It's just for a few months.

B PAIRS **Practice the conversation. Use your own names.**

C PAIRS **Practice the conversation again. Make similar conversations. Talk about a financial decision that you and your partner disagree on.**

WHAT DO YOU THINK?

PAIRS Abe is making big purchases on credit because he's sure that he'll be making more money soon to pay off his credit card debt. Do you think it is OK to spend money you haven't earned yet? Is it OK to have credit card debt? Why or why not?

JOB-SEEKING SKILLS

Prepare for a job interview

@RafikAramayan *Today*
I have an interview next week! Now I have to get ready!

GET READY

Rafik has an interview with CloseFit next week. What information do you think Rafik should try to find out about CloseFit before he goes to the interview?

PREPARE FOR A JOB INTERVIEW

A **To prepare for the interview, Rafik thought of some questions that the interviewer may ask him. Read the questions and add three more questions of your own. Imagine you're interviewing for a job. How would you answer each question?**

Questions the Interviewer May Ask:
1. Why did you leave your previous job?
2. Can you please give me an example of a difficult work situation at your last job, and how you, as a team leader, helped solve the problem?
3. What are your salary expectations?
4.
5.
6.

B **Rafik also thought of some questions to ask the interviewer. Read the questions and add three more of your own.**

Questions I Can Ask the Interviewer:
1. How would you describe a typical week in the software development group at CloseFit?
2. If you offer me this job, how soon would you like me to start?
3. What plans does CloseFit have for future growth?
4.
5.
6.

C **What questions shouldn't a person ask during a job interview?**

_____

_____

_____

_____

PUT YOUR IDEAS TO WORK

PAIRS Compare your questions. Select the best questions and share them with the class.

GRAMMAR

In this unit, you studied:

- Placement of direct and indirect objects
- Modals of possibility and conclusion

See page 151 for your Grammar Review.

VOCABULARY See page 160 for the Unit 7 Vocabulary.

Vocabulary Learning Strategy: Write personal sentences

A Choose 10 words from the list. In your notebook, write sentences about yourself or your opinions on something with the words.

> I'm annoyed by office gossip.
> I work hard, but I'm not a workaholic.

B Underline the vocabulary words in Exercise A.

SPELLING See page 160 for the Unit 7 Vocabulary.

CLASS **Choose 10 words for a spelling test.**

LISTENING PLUS

A Watch each video. Write the story of Ben's day on a separate piece of paper.

> Ben is meeting Amaya for coffee. Ben tells Amaya about his asking his boss
> for a promotion. Amaya wants Ben to volunteer at the Family Day event.

B PAIRS **Review the conversation in Lesson 4.** (See page 94.)
Role play the conversation for the class.

NOW I CAN

PAIRS **See page 89 for the Unit 7 Goals.** Check ☑ the things you can do.
Underline the things you want to study more. Tell your partner.

> I can _____. I need more practice with _____.

8 Lena Reports

MY GOALS

☐ Report housing problems

☐ Give a progress report

☐ Read a return policy

☐ Call about returning merchandise

☐ Answer common interview questions

Go to MyEnglishLab for more practice after each lesson.

Lena Panich

Lena   *Today*
Things have not been going smoothly lately. I have to make a few phone calls to make things right.

103

1

Report housing problems

GET READY TO WATCH

Lena has a conversation with her landlord about a problem. Have you ever had to report a housing problem? What happened?

WATCH

◼◀ **Watch the video. Complete the sentences with the words from the box.**

> sewer   handyman   low   pipes   neighbors   report

1. At first, Lena's landlord told her to call the _____.
2. Lena found out that her _____ have the same problem.
3. In Lena's building, everyone on the first floor has clogged _____.
4. Marcos thinks there's a problem with the main _____ connection.
5. Lena doesn't want to leave her apartment because the rent is _____.
6. Marcos thinks Lena should _____ her landlord.

CONVERSATION

A ◼◀ **Watch part of the video. Complete the conversation.**

Marcos: Is everything OK?

Lena: I was talking to my landlord. He said that I finally have a plumber on the way.

Marcos: You're still having plumbing problems?

Lena: Yes. Our sink has been stopped up for ages. The water _____ really, really slowly.

Marcos: In the kitchen or the bathroom?

Lena: Both! We've tried drain cleaner, and my husband even _____ a piece of pipe, but nothing works.

Marcos: Isn't fixing the sink your landlord's job?

Lena: It is, but he resists doing anything for the apartment.

> **Pronunciation Note**
>
> Notice the three different vowel sounds in *ran* /æ/, *up* /ʌ/, and *job* /ɑ/. Open your mouth and put your tongue behind your bottom teeth for /æ/. Open your mouth wide for /ɑ/ and just a little for /ə/.
>
> ◀)) **Listen and repeat.**
>
> | /æ/ | having | landlord | handyman |
> | /ʌ/ | husband | plumber | nothing |
> | /ɑ/ | problem | stopped | blocked |

B PAIRS **Practice the conversation.**

C PAIRS **Practice the conversation again. Make similar conversations. Talk about a housing problem.**

WHAT DO YOU THINK?

PAIRS Lena's landlord resists calling repair people, but Lena doesn't want to report him because she's afraid he will raise her rent. Should she report him? Why or why not?

STUDY Reported Speech

Direct Speech: Statements	Reported Speech: Statements
She said, "The sink **is** clogged up."	She said (that) the sink **was** clogged up.
She told her husband, "I **spoke** to the landlord."	She told her husband (that) she **had spoken** to the landlord.

Direct Speech: Imperatives	Reported Speech: Imperatives
He told her, "Turn off the water."	He told her to turn off the water.
He said, "Please wait for the plumber to arrive."	He asked her to wait for the plumber to arrive.
He said, "Don't turn on the heat."	He said not to turn on the heat.

> **Grammar Note**
>
> In informal English, the verb in the reported speech often does not change to the past, especially when it refers to something that's still true: "He **said** that I finally **have** a plumber on the way."

 ## PRACTICE

A Read the statements in direct speech. Complete the reported speech statements. Use formal English.

1. Lena said, "Our kitchen sink is clogged up."

   Lena said that their kitchen sink _____was_____ clogged up.

2. Marcos told Lena, "Your landlord sounds awful."

   Marcos told Lena that _____ landlord _____ awful.

3. Marcos told her, "You have rights."

   Marcos told her _____.

4. She said, "I don't want to complain."

   She said _____.

B Imagine that a plumber gives you the following advice for taking care of your plumbing. On a separate piece of paper, rewrite each imperative as reported speech. Use the reporting verb in parentheses.

1. "Pay attention to your drains." (tell)   *He told me to pay attention to my drains.*
2. "Pour boiling water down the drain once a month." (tell)
3. "Put a screen over the drain." (say)
4. "Don't throw paper towels into the toilet." (tell)
5. "Call me as soon as you have a problem." (ask)

WHAT ABOUT YOU?

PAIRS Write a short conversation in which a tenant calls a landlord about a housing problem. Meet with another pair and read your conversation. Then report what you heard.

The tenant said the refrigerator wasn't working.

UNIT 8   **105**

Identify pertinent information

GET READY

Lena is having trouble with the plumbing at her apartment. It's her landlord's job to fix it. If there are problems at the place where you live, who is responsible for fixing them?

READ

◀)) **Listen and read the article. Which rights did you know already? Which are new to you?**

RENTERS BEWARE!

Adamo moved out of his apartment nine months before his lease expired. "I had no choice," he said, "I was starting a new job in another part of the city." He paid rent on two apartments for nine months. His former landlord didn't advertise that his old apartment was available. In fact, he didn't seem to do anything. Adamo said, "He made no effort to try to find a new tenant to replace me." Adamo paid more than he should have. If he had known the rights he has as a renter, he could have saved over $10,000 dollars. "It was an expensive mistake," he said.

Many renters aren't aware that they have rights. Some rights prevent landlords from taking advantage of a situation. Other rights ensure an apartment is in good condition. It's a good idea to be familiar with the renter's rights. Some of the most common are listed here.

Right 1: Many states require landlords to search for a new tenant so they don't have to charge the renter the remaining months left on their lease. When a new renter is found, the one who moved is only responsible for the months that the apartment or house is empty.

Right 2: Rental property must be habitable, which means it needs to be safe, clean, and in good living condition. Apartments, for example, must have utilities, such as heat, water, and electricity. Everything must be in working condition and built well.

Right 3: Renters have the right to have maintenance and repairs made quickly by the landlord. If the landlord can't, then there should be a special clause in the lease that allows renters to have repairs made on their own. They don't have to pay on their own, though. The cost of repairs can be deducted from the rent that month.

Right 4: In most states, landlords are only allowed to enter for emergencies or for repairs. No one else is allowed to enter for any reason. Additionally, landlords cannot enter your propery for repairs without 24 hours' notice.

Right 5: Renters can't lose their security deposit for items that are "normal wear and tear." For example, carpet gets worn and dusty from "normal" use, such as walking or from furniture being placed on it. Those are not reasons to not return your security deposit. In some states, landlords are required to provide a detailed list of what is being deducted from the deposit.

Before signing a lease, go over your rights as a renter with your potential landlord. Don't make the same mistake Adamo made.

AFTER YOU READ

Read the Reading Skill. Read the article again. Complete the statements with information from the article.

Reading Skill

Not all information in a reading is important. **Identifying pertinent information** helps you remember and understand main ideas.

1. Landlords have to _____ so the old tenant doesn't have to pay for the months when the rental property is empty.

2. An apartment that is habitable is _____.

3. Renters have the right to have maintenance done by _____ and it should be done _____.

4. Landlords have to give _____ before entering the property for _____.

5. Normal "wear and tear" is not a reason to not get your _____ back.

VOCABULARY STUDY Synonyms

Build Your Vocabulary

A **synonym** is a word that has the same meaning as another word. For example: *tiny = small*.

Read the Build Your Vocabulary note. Find synonyms in the article for each of the underlined words.

1. It's important to know your rights as a renter. (= _____)

2. This rental property is not livable. It has no water or electricity, and it's not safe. (= _____)

3. Renters don't have to pay for repairs themselves. The cost from repairs can be taken away from the rent that month. (= _____)

4. If you move out of your apartment before your lease ends, your landlord is required to look for a new renter. (= _____)

5. There is a unique clause in the lease that requires the landlord to give 24 hours' notice before entering a property. (= _____)

WHAT DO YOU THINK?

GROUPS What other rights do you think tenants should have?

ON THE WEB

For more information about this topic, go online and search "renter's rights." Report back to the class.

Give a progress report

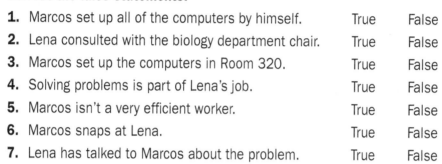

GET READY TO WATCH

Lena is reporting on the progress of a new employee. What are some positive and negative things she might say about him?

WATCH

 A ◼◀ Watch the video. Were your guesses correct?

 B ◼◀ Watch the video again. Read the statements. Circle *True* or *False*. Correct the false statements.

1.	Marcos set up all of the computers by himself.	True	False
2.	Lena consulted with the biology department chair.	True	False
3.	Marcos set up the computers in Room 320.	True	False
4.	Solving problems is part of Lena's job.	True	False
5.	Marcos isn't a very efficient worker.	True	False
6.	Marcos snaps at Lena.	True	False
7.	Lena has talked to Marcos about the problem.	True	False

CONVERSATION

 A ◼◀ Watch part of the video. Complete the conversation.

Tom: So how are things _____ with Marcos?

Lena: He's doing OK. After we set up the computers in Room 201, he did Room 203 by himself.

Tom: That's great!

Lena: I asked him to _____ with the biology department chair before he installed any software, and he did that, too.

Tom: Fantastic!

Lena: And as soon as the computers arrived in Room 320, he started setting them up. I didn't even have to ask.

Tom: Sounds like Marcos is going to work out really well.

> **Pronunciation Note**
>
> We break long sentences into shorter thought groups, pausing (stopping) a little between groups. People may choose to pause in different places, but we always pause after a time clause.
>
> ◀))) **Listen and repeat.**
>
> After we set up the computers / in Room 201, / he did Room 203 / by himself.
>
> When people ask questions, / he gets irritated / and snaps at them.

B **PAIRS** Practice the conversation. Use your own names.

C **PAIRS** Practice the conversation again. Make similar conversations. Talk about how things are coming along with your partner's classes or work.

WHAT DO YOU THINK?

PAIRS Why is it hard for Lena to talk about her problem with Marcos? Would you feel the same way? Why or why not?

5

Adverb clauses of time

 STUDY Adverb Clauses of Time

Tom spoke to Marcos **after Lena brought up the problem**.
When the computers arrived, Marcos installed the software.
Lena told Marcos what she thought **before she spoke to Tom**.
As soon as Lena finishes the installation, students can use the computers.
We will keep working **until the computers are ready**.

Grammar Note

- When the adverb clause comes before the main clause, use a comma between the clauses.
- For sentences with a future meaning, use a present tense verb form in the adverb clause.

PRACTICE

A Read the steps in Lena's procedure for installing a new computer.
Then complete the paragraph with *when, before, after*, and *until*.

1. Make sure that nothing is missing from the box.
2. Set up the parts.
3. Connect the keyboard, mouse, and monitor.
4. Check the cords.
5. Turn on the computer.
6. Register the computer.
7. Install software.

(1) ___When___ Lena receives new computers, she makes sure that nothing is missing from the box. (2) _____ she checks the box, she sets up all of the parts. Then she connects the keyboard, mouse, and monitor. She checks all of the cords (3) _____ she turns the computer on. (4) _____ the computer starts up, she connects to the Internet and registers the computer. She doesn't install any software (5) _____ she has finished registering. (6) _____ she finishes installing the software, the computer is ready for students to use.

B On a separate piece of paper, combine each pair of sentences, using the adverb in parentheses. Don't change the order of the sentences. Use a comma if necessary.

1. The computers arrived. Lena called Marcos. (after)

> *After the computers arrived, Lena called Marcos.*

2. Marcos started setting the computers up. They were delivered to Room 320. (as soon as)
3. Tom will speak to Marcos. Tom will go home at 5:00. (before)
4. Marcos gets annoyed. Students ask him questions. (when)
5. Lena will come to work at 8:00 tomorrow. She will see Marcos. (when)

WHAT ABOUT YOU?

GROUPS **Student A:** Make a statement using an adverb clause of time. **Student B:** Make a new statement using either one of Student A's clauses. Either keep the clause as is or make it into a new adverb clause of time. Continue around the group.

Student A: *When I got to school this morning, I bought a cup of coffee.*
Student B: *After I bought the cup of coffee, I did my homework.*
Student C: *I did my homework until class started.*

GET READY

Lena'a colleague Marcos wants to return something he bought online. What are the differences between returning something you bought at a store and something you bought online?

PRACTICAL READING

Read the online return policy. Circle the correct answers.

○ ○ ○   www.acmetech.com

Home   Shop   Categories   My Cart   Check Out   About Us   Search ⌕

RETURN POLICY AND PROCEDURE

ACME Tech will accept items purchased at the ACME Tech online store for exchange or refund within 30 days of the original purchase date unless stated otherwise in the item listing on the website. Desktop and laptop computers and TVs may be returned or exchanged within 14 days of original purchase only. Consumables, such as ink cartridges, bulbs, blank CDs or DVDs, cannot be returned if the package or outer wrapping has been opened in any way. Make sure you have ordered the correct item before you open the package.

You must receive authorization from ACME Tech before returning any product. In order to receive authorization, all products must be in the same condition as when sold and in the original packaging. All returned products are inspected carefully, and any returned product that is not complete or in its original condition will be rejected and you may be charged an additional fee.

When we inspect the returned product, we check for the following:
• The serial number on the product matches the serial number on the package and invoice.
• The product is not damaged in any way.
• All manuals, accessories, and any other parts have been returned.

Once you receive authorization to return the product, package it securely and return by the U.S. mail or any other shipper. It is a good idea to use a shipping method that provides you with package tracking, a delivery confirmation number, and insurance. ACME Tech is not responsible for items that are damaged or lost during return shipping. The customer is responsible for all return shipping charges.

1. ACME Tech will accept a product for return or exchange _____.
   a. if the customer has damaged it
   b. at any time after purchase
   c. with or without prior authorization
   d. if the product is returned in its original packaging and in its original condition

2. ACME Tech recommends that customers ship an item being returned _____.
   a. securely and with a company that provides delivery confirmation and insurance
   b. only by the U.S. mail
   c. as cheaply as possible since the customer pays for shipping
   d. in new packaging

3. A laptop computer purchased at the ACME Tech website can be returned _____.

    a. at any time   **c.** within 14 days of purchase

    b. within 30 days of purchase   **d.** without authorization

4. When ACME Tech receives a returned product, _____.

    a. it provides an authorization number   **c.** it inspects the item carefully

    b. it charges an additional fee   **d.** it pays for the shipping charge

PRACTICAL SPEAKING

A 🔊 **Marcos is discussing his purchase with his sister, Carla. Listen and read the conversation.**

Marcos: My new speakers are not working. I need to return them.

Carla: Can you do that? I thought you bought them more than a month ago.

Marcos: You're right, but these speakers clearly don't work. I'm going to call and see if I can return them even though it's been more than 30 days.

Carla: If they don't want to give you a full refund, try asking for a store credit. You can use the credit to buy something else.

Marcos: That's a good idea. I'll do that.

Carla: Good luck! Let me know what happens.

B PAIRS **Practice the conversation.**

C PAIRS **Look at the return policy again. Role play a similar conversation. Return an item you're not happy with. Talk about the options.**

PRACTICAL LISTENING

🔊 **Listen to the public service announcement from the Federal Trade Commission (FTC). Complete the sentences with the words from the box.**

> arrive   four   keep track   return   reviews   shipped

1. The FTC wants consumers to know about _____ steps that will help them avoid a bad online shopping experience.

2. When thinking about making an online purchase, look for _____ of online vendors by using a search engine.

3. Before making an online order, make sure you understand the refund and _____ policies completely.

4. You should know when your order will be _____ and how long it will take to _____.

5. It is a good idea to _____ of your online purchases by keeping printouts of your order.

WHAT DO YOU THINK?

PAIRS **Read the part of the return policy about "consumables" again. Why do you think ACME Tech will not accept a returned consumable if its package has been opened? Is the policy reasonable? Why or why not?**

7

Explain a process

GET READY

Marcos needs to install an updated version of a computer program. He reads the manual that comes with the program. What kind of information do you expect to find in a computer program manual?

STUDY THE MODEL

A Read the process. What is the first step the writer explains?

INSTALLATION

Thank you for purchasing the updated version of the Safe System Software Program. Follow these steps to install the program on your computer.

Before installation, there are a few things to check. First, make sure your computer has all the system requirements necessary for a successful installation. Additionally, check for earlier versions of the Safe System Software. Those will need to be removed before the new version can be installed.

Then, create any necessary program files. A list of program files is included. In addition, create program folders to store the files on your computer.

Prepare to install the software program. Close the other windows open on your computer. After that, close any programs running on your computer. Now you are ready to install the program.

Insert the CD-ROM into the computer. A window will appear automatically. Click *Install*. Then restart your computer when prompted. The program will be ready to use when the computer restarts.

1A

Writing Tip

Writers use **transition words** to add more information when explaining a process.

additionally	*after that*
in addition	*then*
likewise	*now*
similarly	*plus*
moreover	*besides*

B Read the Writing Tip. Read the process again. Underline the transition words.

c Look at and complete the flowchart the writer used to plan the process.

Installing an updated version of a computer program

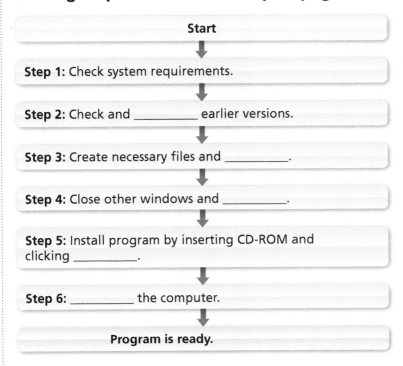

Start

Step 1: Check system requirements.

Step 2: Check and _____ earlier versions.

Step 3: Create necessary files and _____.

Step 4: Close other windows and _____.

Step 5: Install program by inserting CD-ROM and clicking _____.

Step 6: _____ the computer.

Program is ready.

BEFORE YOU WRITE

You're going to write about a process that you are familiar with. Use the flowchart to explain your process.

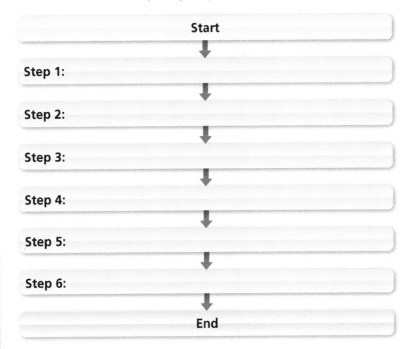

Start

Step 1:

Step 2:

Step 3:

Step 4:

Step 5:

Step 6:

End

WRITE

Review the Model and the Writing Tip. Use the ideas from your flowchart to write about a process.

Call about returning merchandise

GET READY TO WATCH

Lena is calling to return an item that she bought online. Have you ever had to do that? What happened?

WATCH

█◀ Watch the video. Answer the questions.

1. What number does Lena have to press?

2. Why is Lena calling ACME Tech?

3. Why didn't Lena check the headphones before?

4. What does Keith ask Lena to check?

5. Why does Lena get annoyed at Keith's questions?

6. What does Keith offer Lena instead of a refund?

CONVERSATION

 A

█◀ Watch part of the video. Complete the conversation.

Keith: As long as the _____ are in like-new condition, there's no problem. Just complete the return form that came with your package and ship them back. We'll send you a replacement.

Lena: Mmm. I don't want a replacement now. Can't I just get a refund?

Keith: I'm sorry, but we don't give refunds after 30 days.

Lena: But they're _____. I've never used them.

Keith: Well, if you send them back, I can give you a store credit.

Lena: OK, that's fine. I'll do that.

B **PAIRS** Practice the conversation.

C **PAIRS** Practice the conversation again. Make similar conversations. Return an item you ordered online. Talk about the options.

WHAT DO YOU THINK?

PAIRS Is it reasonable for Lena to ask for a refund after she was told it had passed the date? Should it make any difference if the items are defective and unused? Why or why not?

JOB-SEEKING SKILLS

Answer common interview questions

@RafikAramayan *Today*
My interview is in
just a few minutes!
I'm reviewing my notes.
Wish me luck!

GET READY

Rafik is about to have a job interview. What advice would you give him about choosing an outfit for the interview? How should he behave during the interview?

ANSWER COMMON INTERVIEW QUESTIONS

A 🔊 **Listen to the first part of Rafik's interview. Read the statements. Circle *True* or *False*. Correct the false statements.**

1. Rafik is looking for a new job because he was not happy with his salary at his previous job.	True	False
2. When Rafik was appointed as team leader at his previous job, the project was on schedule.	True	False
3. Rafik thinks that his major strength as a team leader was working hard.	True	False
4. Ms. Barrett thinks that Rafik should have more dynamic presentation skills.	True	False
5. If Rafik gets the job, he can start working in two weeks.	True	False

B 🔊 **Listen to the first part of Rafik's interview again. Circle the correct answers.**

1. Why did Rafik leave his job at Aerospace Systems?
   a. He had an argument with his boss.
   b. He didn't have good presentation skills.
   c. The project he was working on was behind schedule and over budget.
   d. The company moved to a different state.

2. Which statement is true about Rafik?
   a. He has very little experience working as a software programmer.
   b. He's a good listener and problem solver.
   c. He has always had great presentation skills.
   d. He lives very close to San Francisco.

3. As a team leader at Aerospace Systems, how did Rafik complete a major project on time?
   a. He improved the way the software developers and engineers communicated with each other.
   b. He laid off 1/3 of the employees in his department.
   c. He made sure the people had good training.
   d. He spent $500,000 to turn the project around.

4. What did Rafik do to improve himself as a team leader?
   a. He made sure he listened to people's problems.
   b. He improved his budgeting skills.
   c. He enrolled in a public speaking class.
   d. He improved his computer programming skills.

PUT YOUR IDEAS TO WORK

GROUPS How did Rafik talk about the area he needed to improve as a team leader? Do you think he did a good job answering that question? What are other ways you can answer a question about a weakness?

GRAMMAR

In this unit, you studied:

- Reported speech: statements and imperatives
- Adverb clauses of time

See page 152 for your Grammar Review.

VOCABULARY   See page 160 for the Unit 8 Vocabulary.

Vocabulary Learning Strategy: Use synonyms

A **Find words from the list with the same meanings as the words below. Fill in the blanks.**

_____annoyed_____ = _____   _____move_____ = _____

_____strange_____ = _____   _____safely_____ = _____

_____examine_____ = _____   _____notice_____ = _____

_____blocked_____ = _____   _____ask_____ = _____

_____ = _____   _____ = _____

B **Circle 5 vocabulary words in Exercise A. Write a sentence with each word.**

SPELLING   See page 160 for the Unit 8 Vocabulary.

CLASS **Choose 10 words for a spelling test.**

LISTENING PLUS

A **Watch each video. Write the story of Lena's day on a separate piece of paper.**

Lena has been having problems with her apartment. She just finished talking
with her landlord. She's telling Marcos about the problems.

B **PAIRS Review the conversation in Lesson 1. (See page 104.)**
Role play the conversation for the class.

NOW I CAN

PAIRS See page 103 for the Unit 8 Goals. Check ☑ the things you can do.
Underline the things you want to study more. Tell your partner.

> I can _____. I need more practice with _____.

9

Emily's Teamwork

MY GOALS

☐ Give instructions

☐ Read a lease

☐ Talk about moving

☐ Work as a team

☐ Ask questions at a job interview

Go to MyEnglishLab for more practice after each lesson.

Emily Campos

Emily *Today*
It's a great experience to work with others. You just need to be flexible and open-minded.

117

Give instructions

GET READY TO WATCH

Emily is giving Gina instructions to do things for her. Do you usually write down instructions, or do you try to remember them?

WATCH

■◀ **Watch the video. Read the statements. Circle *True* or *False*. Correct the false statements.**

1.	Gina writes down the instructions that Emily gives her.	True	False
2.	Diana needs to fill out a receipt for the key.	True	False
3.	Gina needs to take out the trash in one of the classrooms.	True	False
4.	The morning custodian will clean the rooms.	True	False
5.	Gina is going to pick up campus maps at the Copy Center.	True	False
6.	Gina remembers that she needs to take a key to the business department.	True	False

CONVERSATION

A ■◀ **Watch part of the video. Complete the conversation.**

Emily: Can you help me out with some _____ today?

Gina: Of course. What do you need?

Emily: You'd better write this down—it's a lot to remember.

Gina: It's OK, I've got it.

Emily: OK . . . Well, first, drop this key off at the Business Department, Dean Spelling's office. It's for Diana, the dean's assistant.

Gina: I think I can handle that.

Emily: There's a little form in here that she needs to fill out—it's a receipt. Just put it on my desk when you get back.

Gina: No problem. You can _____ me. What's next?

B PAIRS **Practice the conversation.**

C PAIRS **Practice the conversation again. Make similar conversations. Give your partner instructions to do certain things for you.**

> **Pronunciation Note**
>
> In most phrasal verbs, both the verb and particle are stressed. If there is a noun object, the noun may be stressed instead of a particle. If there is a pronoun object, the pronoun is not stressed.
>
> ◀)) **Listen and repeat.**
> You'd better **write** this **down**.
>
> **Drop** this **key** off.
>
> **Pick** it **up** and **throw** it **away**.

WHAT DO YOU THINK?

PAIRS Why do you think Gina doesn't want to make a list? Now that she has forgotten some of her instructions, what should she do?

GRAMMAR

Phrasal verbs

STUDY Phrasal Verbs

Separable Phrasal Verbs	Inseparable Phrasal Verbs
Write down the information.	You can **count on** Gina.
Write the information **down**.	You can **count on** her.
Write it **down**.	

(See p. 156 for a list of separable and inseparable phrasal verbs.)

Grammar Note

- A phrasal verb contains a verb and a particle. Particles are words such as *up*, *down*, *on*, *off*, *in*, and *out*.
- When the object of a separable phrasal verb is a pronoun, it must come before the particle.

PRACTICE

A

Rewrite the sentences. Use a pronoun for the direct object.

1. Gina is going to drop off the key. *Gina is going to drop it off.*

2. Gina doesn't need to take out trash. _____

3. Emily is going to pass out the maps. _____

4. Diana needs to fill out the form. _____

5. The dean counts on Diana to plan conferences. _____

6. Gina didn't write down the information. _____

7. Gina is going to help out Emily today. _____

8. Did Gina look up the room numbers? _____

B

Read the paragraph. Underline the phrasal verbs. Then write the correct phrasal verb next to each definition.

Office assistants may have a wide variety of duties. They often help out anyone in the office who has too much work to do. Sometimes they pick up or drop off items for their supervisors. Sometimes they fill out routine office forms. When people run out of supplies, the office assistants put in an order. If the receptionist is out, an assistant may need to answer phones and note down messages. Managers count on office assistants to keep the office organized.

1. assist: _____*help out*_____   5. collect: _____

2. deliver: _____   6. submit: _____

3. write: _____   7. use all: _____

4. complete: _____   8. trust: _____

WHAT ABOUT YOU?

PAIRS Write a conversation or a paragraph using 6 phrasal verbs. Read your work to another pair. As you listen to the other pair, write down the 6 phrasal verbs you hear.

GET READY

Emily's friend Paula just moved into a two-bedroom apartment. She signed a one-year lease before she moved in. What is usually included in an apartment rental agreement?

PRACTICAL READING

A **Look at Emily's lease. Why is it important to read a lease carefully?**

RENTAL AGREEMENT

This agreement is entered into this __1__ day of _April_ , _2014_ , between _Irene Tam_ (hereafter "Landlord"), and _Paula Sullivan_ (hereafter "Tenant"). The Landlord and Tenant agree that the Landlord rents to the Tenant for residential use apartment No. __47__ at _1500 Sherman Drive, Long Beach, California_ for the term of __12__ months, beginning on _April 1, 2014_ . The Tenant agrees to pay $ _1,225_ rent per month beginning _April 1, 2014_ .

All rental payments are due in advance, on or before the first day of each month. All rental payments received 10 days after the due date will have a $40 late fee added to them.

The Tenant also agrees that:
- No pets are allowed.
- The Tenant will pay for all utilities except hot and cold water, sewer, and trash collection.
- The premises will only be occupied by the Tenant.
- The Tenant may not sublet the apartment or any part of the apartment.
- The Tenant will keep the premises clean and safe.
- The Tenant will not perform any repairs or alterations without the Landlord's prior written agreement.

A security deposit in the amount of _$1,225_ has been paid by the Tenant. The Landlord may use some or all of the security deposit to remedy any damages caused by the Tenant or the Tenant's guests or to clean the apartment at the termination of lease. If the cost of repairing the apartment is more than the security deposit, the Tenant is liable for the difference.

The Landlord has the right to enter the premises as permitted by law to make necessary or agreed repairs and to make inspections. The Landlord will give the Tenant 24 hours' notice before entry except in an emergency.

The Landlord is not responsible for any damages to the Tenant or any of the Tenant's property caused by other persons, including theft, burglary, vandalism or other crimes. The Landlord is not responsible for any damages to the Tenant or any of the Tenant's property caused by fire, flood, rain, ice, snow, or other occurrences.

Signed: _Irene Tam_   Date: _April 1, 2014_
　　　　　Landlord

　　　　　Paula Sullivan   Date: _April 1, 2014_
　　　　　Tenant

B Look at the lease again. Read the statements. Circle *True* or *False*.
Correct the false statements.

1. Irene Tam is the landlord of the apartment building.	True	False
2. Paula Sullivan has to pay for all of her utility bills.	True	False
3. To make extra money, Paula can rent the bedroom she isn't using to a college student looking for a place to stay.	True	False
4. Paula will be able to get a dog.	True	False
5. The landlord can enter Paula's apartment to inspect the property or make repairs without giving 24 hours' notice in an emergency.	True	False
6. The landlord must pay to fix a tenant's car if it is damaged by water due to a flood.	True	False

PRACTICAL SPEAKING

A ◀))) **Paula is discussing the lease with the landlord. Listen and read the conversation.**

Ms. Tam: Do you have any questions about the lease?

Paula: Actually, I do. Can I rent one bedroom out to a student after my oldest son goes to college?

Ms. Tam: I'm sorry. The lease doesn't allow a tenant to sublet the apartment or any part of the apartment.

Paula: I see.

B PAIRS **Practice the conversation.**

C PAIRS **Look at the lease again. Role play a similar conversation between a landlord and a tenant. Ask and answer questions about the lease.**

PRACTICAL LISTENING

◀))) **Listen to the radio commercial about rental apartments.
Answer the questions.**

1. Is the Blue Train station near or far away from the Village Rental Apartments?

2. What type of apartments are available for rent at the Village Rental Apartments?

3. How will living at the Village Rental Apartments give you more time for reading?

4. What three features of the Village Rental Apartments are meant to help you relax?

5. When will the newly renovated apartments be available?

WHAT DO YOU THINK?

GROUPS The lease does not include the landlord's responsibilities. Make a list of things you think the landlord should be responsible for. Share your list with the class.

LISTENING AND SPEAKING

Talk about moving

GET READY TO WATCH

Emily is tired because she just moved. How often have you moved? How do you feel about moving?

WATCH

◀ **Watch the video. Circle the correct answers.**

1. Emily's move was difficult because _____.
   a. she was up all night partying
   b. her sons didn't help
   c. her new apartment is smaller than her old home

2. Emily had acquired a lot of belongings because _____.
   a. she doesn't like to have garage sales
   b. she lived in her old home for 15 years
   c. her sons put a lot of things in the garage

3. Emily didn't want to have another garage sale because _____.
   a. it was too much work
   b. they didn't make enough money
   c. her sons didn't enjoy it

CONVERSATION

A ◀ **Watch part of the video.
Complete the conversation.**

Sam: How did the move go?

Emily: It was a _____.

Sam: Aren't your sons helping you out?

Emily: They're helping. But we're moving from a
_____-sized house into a
much smaller apartment. It's not easy.

Sam: Oh, sorry about that.

Emily: Don't be sorry. We moved into an apartment because I don't want to spend
my weekends doing yard work and household maintenance. Since my boys
are both leaving for college soon, this seemed like a good time.

B PAIRS **Practice the conversation.**

C PAIRS **Practice the conversation again. Make similar conversations.
Talk about why you moved.**

Pronunciation Note

Most two-syllable nouns and adjectives
are stressed on the first syllable.
Two-syllable verbs are often stressed
on the second syllable.

◀))) **Listen and repeat.**

(noun)	**night**mare	**col**lege	**prof**it
(adjective)	**de**cent	**sor**ry	**hap**py
(verb)	un**pack**	ac**quire**	en**joy**

WHAT DO YOU THINK?

PAIRS Like many people, Emily has acquired a lot of belongings that she doesn't need.
Do you think this is a serious problem? Why or why not?

STUDY Adverb Clauses of Reason

She moved **because she wanted more convenience**.
Since she has two children, she lives in a three-bedroom apartment.
Now that her sons are older, they can help out with the move.

Grammar Note

In spoken English, we often use adverb clauses of reason on their own as short answers: *Because I'm tired.* In written English, adverb clauses must be connected to main clauses.

PRACTICE

A Match the sentence parts.

_f_ **1.** Some people like moving

_____ **2.** Since moving requires packing and unpacking,

_____ **3.** People often move

_____ **4.** Some people pay a moving company to pack

_____ **5.** Because Americans move so often,

_____ **6.** It's a good idea to start packing early

a. because they get a job in a new location.

b. they often don't know their neighbors.

c. because it makes the move much easier.

d. it can be exhausting.

e. since it can take longer than you expect.

f. because they like to live in a new place.

B On a separate piece of paper, combine each pair of sentences, using the word(s) in parentheses. Don't change the order of the sentences. Use a comma if necessary.

1. Emily decided to move. She doesn't want to take care of a house. (because)

> *Emily decided to move because she doesn't want to take care of a house.*

2. They had a lot of unnecessary belongings. They had a garage sale. (since)

3. They are in a smaller home. They can't acquire things the way they used to. (now that)

4. She won't need to do yard work anymore. She's living in an apartment. (now that)

5. She needs to save money. Her sons are going to college soon. (since)

6. Her sons are older. They help out a lot. (because)

WHAT ABOUT YOU?

PAIRS Work together to write 6 questions with *Why*. Write questions your classmates know the answer to—for example, *Why did you move to the United States?* or *Why does the teacher give tests?* Sit with another pair. Ask and answer each other's questions, using complete sentences.

Identify fact versus opinion

GET READY

Emily helps with event planning in her younger son's school. They are publishing a newsletter about how parents can be involved in their children's education. Do you think it is important for parents to be involved in their children's education? Why?

READI

◀))) **Listen and read the article. In what ways can parents get involved?**

Be an A+ Parent

Everyone wants their children to get an A+ report card. One of the best ways to help your kids is to be an A+ parent. Research shows that children with involved parents tend to get better grades, have more positive attitudes, and experience fewer problems in school.

A+ parents stay in touch with teachers. Give teachers your contact information within the first few weeks of school. Let the teachers know you want to hear both the good things and the bad things. It may be hard to hear the bad news, but being open to it will make teachers less hesitant to contact you about problems.

It is a good idea to schedule time to get involved. People think it may be difficult to have frequent individual meetings. Consider joining the Parent Teacher Association (PTA). Being a member of the PTA will keep you updated on school issues and will offer opportunities to see teachers outside of school hours.

Another easy way to be involved is to volunteer once or twice a year. Some good volunteer work includes reading stories at the school library, coaching one of the sports teams, or accompanying children on a field trip. A lot of parents have participated, and they think it was fun.

Being involved extends beyond school hours. A+ parents are involved at home as well. They set homework time and study hours. They attend their children's extracurricular activities, such as the school play or football game. We know a lot of people might disagree, but surveys have shown that students love having their parents there.

Last, but not least, you should show your kids that you think reading is important. Let them see you reading often or read the same books your kids are reading. Ask them questions about the books they are reading. Schedule time to discuss ideas in the books. Arrange trips to the library, the bookmobile, or literacy events. If you show that reading is important to you, your kids will think it's important, too.

By doing these few simple things, parents are more likely to help their kids succeed throughout their schooling. Everyone can be an A+ parent.

Reading Skill

Writers often include both facts and opinions. A **fact** is something that can be proven or is true. An **opinion** is what someone believes or thinks. As you read, be careful to **identify facts versus opinions**.

AFTER YOU READ

**Read the Reading Skill. Read the article again. Then read the statements.
Write *F* (fact) or *O* (opinion).**

_____ **1.** Research shows that children with involved parents tend to get better grades.

_____ **2.** It may be hard to hear the bad news.

_____ **3.** It is a good idea to schedule time to get involved.

_____ **4.** Parents should be involved at home as well.

_____ **5.** Surveys have shown that children like having their parents attend events.

_____ **6.** You should show your kids that you think reading is important.

VOCABULARY STUDY Antonyms

Build Your Vocabulary

An **antonym** is a word that means the opposite of another word.
For example: *best ≠ worst*.

**Read the Build Your Vocabulary note. Search the article for an
antonym for each underlined word.**

1. There are some easy (≠ _____) ways to get involved at your
children's school.

2. Involved parents can reduce their children's negative (≠ _____)
attitudes towards school.

3. Don't wait until the last (≠ _____) day of school to talk
to teachers.

4. Teachers are ready (≠ _____) to talk to parents who are open
to hearing good and bad news from school.

5. The PTA has group (≠ _____) meetings to keep parents updated
on school issues.

6. Many people agree (≠ _____) that children are happy when their
parents attend extracurricular events.

WHAT DO YOU THINK?

GROUPS What are other ways parents can
get involved in their children's education?
Share your ideas with the class.

ON THE WEB
For more information about this topic, go online and search "parent involvement." Report back to the class.

Write a comparison-and-contrast paragraph

GET READY

Emily is writing a short article for the PTA newsletter about two after-school programs. What kind of information do you expect to find in the article?

STUDY THE MODEL

A **Read the article. What do both programs have in common?**

Welcome to Rosedale High School in the Wood Hazel School District. Rosedale maintains high academic standards in its curriculum, but it also has excellent after-school programs—an arts program and a sports program.

Both programs run from approximately 4 P.M. until 5:30 P.M, which makes them ideal for students whose parents work. Moreover, they are both free of charge. The arts program is led by Mr. Michaels, a school teacher. Likewise, the sports program is managed by Coach Williams. While the programs are both in the same school, they are different in some ways. The arts program runs throughout the academic year, from September until June, whereas the sports program is shorter, running from September until May, and there is no program in December. The arts program is much smaller, with only 50 students. In contrast, the sports program is much larger, with over 120 students. The sports program is well established; in fact, it has existed since the school opened in 1985. Unlike the sports program, the arts program is much newer, having just started in 2010. Both programs are highly successful. Rosedale holds top honors in art shows with over 35% of the students winning ribbons at the city's art fair. Similarly, the sports program holds top honors in athletics with 70% of its teams winning a championship within the past three years.

Rosedale is proud to continue the tradition of strong and valuable after-school programming again this year. Talk to your children and see if they prefer arts or sports. Enroll them today.

Writing Tip

When **comparing** and **contrasting** two things, writers use certain words to express similarities and differences.

Comparison (show similarities)	Contrast (show differences)
both	whereas/while
as well/not either	different
similarly	in contrast
likewise	however
like	unlike

B **Read the Writing Tip. Read the article again. Underline the comparison words. Circle the contrast words.**

C **Look at and complete the Venn diagram the writer used to plan the writing.**

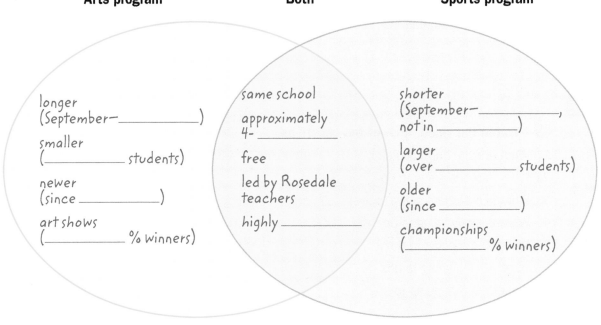

Arts program	Both	Sports program
longer (September—_____)	same school	shorter (September—_____, not in _____)
smaller (_____ students)	approximately 4-_____	larger (over _____ students)
newer (since _____)	free	older (since _____)
art shows (_____ % winners)	led by Rosedale teachers	championships (_____ % winners)
	highly _____	

BEFORE YOU WRITE

You're going to write a comparison-and-contrast paragraph about two cities you are familiar with. Use the Venn diagram below to plan your paragraph.

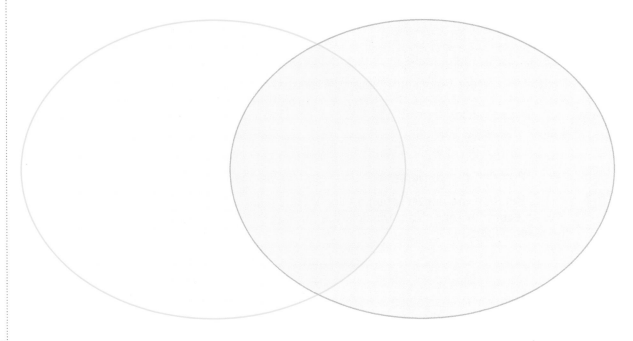

WRITE

Review the Model and the Writing Tip. Use the ideas from your Venn diagram to write your comparison-and-contrast paragraph.

Work as a team

GET READY TO WATCH

Emily, Gina, and Amaya are dividing up the tasks
for a school event. Have you ever had to work with
others to plan something? What happened?

WATCH

◼◀ **Watch the video. Answer the questions.**

1. What are Jim and Koji going to do for the event?

2. What is Maria going to do?

3. What is a student going to oversee?

4. What is Emily going to do?

5. What is Ben going to do?

6. What is Gina going to do?

7. What is Amaya going to do?

CONVERSATION

A ◼◀ **Watch part of the video. Complete the conversation.**

Emily: So, are we all set for Saturday?

Amaya: I think so. Have you arranged for the tables?

Emily: I have. Jim and Koji will be bringing them over first thing, so the students can start
            setting up their _____ any time after 10 A.M.

Amaya: Great. I'll put Maria in charge of organizing the student groups.

Emily: Is someone monitoring cleanup? They need to take down the
            _____ by 7:00.

Amaya: I've got a student _____ that. He'll make sure
            everyone clears off the tables in time.

B PAIRS **Practice the conversation. Use your own names.**

C PAIRS **Practice the conversation again. Make similar conversations.
Plan an event for your class. Discuss the arrangements and divide
the responsibilities.**

WHAT DO YOU THINK?

PAIRS Amaya is in charge of a school event, but she has delegated all of
the specific tasks to other people. Is this a good plan? Why or why not?

@RafikAramayan *Today*
I just finished my interview. I think I did well. Fingers crossed!

GET READY

Rafik has prepared several questions to ask the interviewer. Imagine you are Rafik. What questions would you ask?

ASK QUESTIONS AT A JOB INTERVIEW

A ◀))) **Listen to the second part of Rafik's interview. Read the statements. Circle *True* or *False*. Correct the false statements.**

1.	The first question Rafik asked is about the schedule.	True	False
2.	The first thing Rafik would do at the position is to reorganize the team.	True	False
3.	Ms. Barrett describes Rafik as a people person.	True	False
4.	Rafik would like to advance his career at CloseFit.	True	False
5.	Rafik forgot to bring a list of references with him.	True	False
6.	Rafik will be the last person to be interviewed.	True	False

B ◀))) **Listen to the second part of Rafik's interview again. Circle the correct answers.**

1. What does Ms. Barrett identify as the largest problem facing the software development team?
   a. The Virtual Fitting Room project won't be ready for another five years.
   b. There are still several more people to interview.
   c. They need more money for the Virtual Fitting Room project.
   d. The software development team has lost its momentum.

2. How would Rafik motivate the team?
   a. He would meet with the project manager to go over the tasks.
   b. He would help the team members solve problems.
   c. He would make sure each team member takes ownership of the project.
   d. He would make sure there is no overtime.

3. Which of the statements is true?
   a. Rafik has not done any research about the company.
   b. This position does not require hands-on programming skills.
   c. Rafik thinks people trust him as a person but not as a leader.
   d. Rafik doesn't like overtime.

4. Which of the matters *doesn't* Rafik discuss with Ms. Barrett?
   a. a typical day in the position
   b. salary
   c. the schedule
   d. opportunities for promotion

PUT YOUR IDEAS TO WORK

GROUPS Do you think Rafik asked good questions? Imagine you are Rafik. What other questions would you ask? Share your ideas with the class.

GRAMMAR

In this unit, you studied:

- Phrasal verbs
- Adverb clauses of reason

See page 153 for your Grammar Review.

VOCABULARY See page 161 for the Unit 9 Vocabulary.

Vocabulary Learning Strategy: Use familiar words to learn new words

A Find words from the list that contain familiar words within the words. Fill in the blanks.

_____ errand _____ = err + and   _____ = here + _____

_____ = sub + _____   _____ = _____ + see

_____ = _____ + um   _____ = out + _____

_____ = owner + _____   _____ = _____ + shoot

_____ = _____ + mare   _____ = dele + _____

B Circle 5 vocabulary words in Exercise A. Write a sentence with each word.

SPELLING See page 161 for the Unit 9 Vocabulary.

CLASS Choose 10 words for a spelling test.

LISTENING PLUS

A Watch each video. Write the story of Emily's day on a separate piece of paper.

> Gina offers to help Emily with some errands. Emily gives Gina a lot of instructions, but Gina doesn't write them down. Gina forgets some of the instructions.

B **PAIRS** Review the conversation in Lesson 1. (See page 118.)
Role play the conversation for the class.

NOW I CAN

PAIRS See page 117 for the Unit 9 Goals. Check ☑ the things you can do.
Underline the things you want to study more. Tell your partner.

> I can _____. I need more practice with _____.

10 Sam Looks Forward

MY GOALS

- ☐ Explore career opportunities
- ☐ Talk about wishes and dreams
- ☐ Read a course schedule
- ☐ Set goals
- ☐ Write a follow-up message after a job interview

Go to MyEnglishLab for more practice after each lesson.

Sam Wu
Sam   *Today*
They say, "The longest journey begins with a single step." I guess it's time to get started!

Explore career opportunities

GET READY TO WATCH

Sam is visiting the university career counselor. Have you ever spoken to a career or educational counselor? What happened?

WATCH

◼◀ **Watch the video. Read the statements. Circle *True* or *False*. Correct the false statements.**

1. Sam has been a security guard for ten years.	True	False
2. Sam knows what kind of job he would like.	True	False
3. Sam is really nervous about the test.	True	False
4. The test will tell Sam which job to apply for.	True	False
5. Sam enjoys talking to and helping people.	True	False
6. Tonya thinks that Sam might enjoy teaching.	True	False
7. Sam could finish a four-year degree very quickly.	True	False

CONVERSATION

 A ◼◀ **Watch part of the video. Complete the conversation.**

Tonya: So, Sam. Can you tell me what you like about your

_____ job?

Sam: I like the variety. I get to talk to new people every day.

Tonya: OK. Now what activities, on the job or in your everyday life,

give you a sense of _____?

Sam: Well, sometimes students have little problems, and I help them sort things out. I really like doing that.

Tonya: Interesting. Have you thought about teaching? Or counseling?

B PAIRS **Practice the conversation. Use your own names.**

C PAIRS **Practice the conversation again. Make similar conversations. Talk about what gives you a sense of fulfillment. Explore career opportunities.**

WHAT DO YOU THINK?

 PAIRS The counselor says she knows someone who graduated from law school at 50 years old. Do you think most people can make big changes later in life? Why or why not?

STUDY Embedded Questions

Direct Questions	Embedded Questions
Wh- Questions	
What time is the appointment?	Can you tell me **what time the appointment is**?
What does Sam want?	Can you explain **what Sam wants**?
When did you start working here?	I'd like to know **when you started working here**.
Yes/No Questions	
Do I need a college degree?	I wonder **if/whether I need a college degree**.
Does class start at 8 or 8:30?	I'm not sure **if/whether class starts at 8 or 8:30**.

Grammar Note

Embedded questions are generally more polite than direct questions.

PRACTICE

A **Put the words in the correct order to make embedded questions. Add punctuation.**

1. the counselor / do you know / said / what   _Do you know what the counselor said?_

2. the test / how long / I wonder / will take   _____

3. my options / are / I don't / what / know   _____

4. any / have taken / I'd like / college classes / to know / if you

   _____

5. explain / my career / change / could you / how / I can

   _____

B **On a separate piece of paper, rewrite each direct question as an embedded question. Use the phrase in parentheses.**

1. Where is the counseling office? (Can you tell me)

   Can you tell me where the counseling office is?

2. Which careers pay well? (I wonder)

3. How long does it take to get a BA? (Do you know)

4. Does she have a GED? (Can you tell me)

5. What did he study at college? (I don't know)

6. When will Sam start taking classes? (I'm not sure)

7. Is it difficult to pass this test? (I'd like to know)

WHAT ABOUT YOU?

PAIRS Imagine that you are a new student. Write 5 embedded questions about your class or campus. Include at least 1 *yes/no* question and 3 different question words. Ask and answer your questions with a partner. Then find a new partner and ask your questions again.

Do you know where the cafeteria is?

3 Interpret the author's point of view

GET READY

Sam plans to go back to school while working. He needs to balance school and work with his personal life. How do you balance school and your personal life?

READ

◀))) **Listen and read the article. How has the work/life balance changed?**

Are you vacationing or are you working?

When was the last time you took a vacation? Did you check your email while on vacation? Did you check the messages in your voicemail?

The balance between work and life seems to have changed. Nowadays more and more people are sacrificing vacation time for work. Even when they are on vacation, they take their work with them. Now that technology is so portable, people can check their email on laptops and their voicemail on cell phones or log into work servers from around the world.

Let's analyze this phenomenon. "It has its advantages," said Mario Romano. "It's convenient and efficient. If I check my email while I'm on

vacation, there is a lot less email to read when I get back to the office." Peter Cullen has a different reason for checking in at the office—teamwork. "I don't want to leave coworkers stranded. We're part of a team, and I don't want them to fall behind while I'm on vacation with my family." Some workers are more worried about losing their jobs if they don't check email or call in for messages while they're on vacation. Martina Portifenko explained that there is no excuse for not calling in. "With cell phones and laptops, checking in is easy, and now bosses expect it more than they did before."

All these reasons sound legitimate. However, does it have to be that way? Is working while vacationing a necessary evil? Or is it a workaholic's excuse? Is it the fear of job loss that has driven the work/life balance into a state of imbalance? Or is it the convenience and efficiency of technology that caused it? In the end, I believe everyone chooses their own work/life balance.

When does technology switch from being a blessing into being a curse? Mario Romano's wife, Angelica, says he is really on the computer more than he is with the family. "It's an excessive amount of time. Everyone is at the pool. He's there physically, but he's not there mentally because he's on his cell phone or his computer." Many workers agree that they want to take time off to maintain a better work/life balance. Unfortunately technology has made it hard to do so.

Reading Skill

Writers don't always express their opinions obviously. **Interpreting the author's point of view** helps you determine if the writer is in favor of or against something.

AFTER YOU READ

Read the Reading Skill on page 134. Read the article again. Circle the correct answers.

1. What's the author's point of view on the work/life balance today?
   a. The imbalance between work and life cannot be avoided.
   b. The balance between work and life is no longer recommended.
   c. The imbalance between work and life is an unfortunate trend.

2. How does the author feel about the impact of technology on the work/life balance?
   a. Technology is the reason that there is a work/life imbalance.
   b. Technology positively impacts the work/life balance since it is portable.
   c. Technology is saving employees' time later.

3. Which of the statements do you think the writer would agree with?
   a. Working while vacationing is convenient and efficient and therefore should be encouraged.
   b. Technology in general does more harm than good.
   c. Maintaining a better work/life balance is a personal choice.

VOCABULARY STUDY Word Families

Build Your Vocabulary

A **word family** is a group of words that have the same root. Adding a suffix changes the form of the word, but the family is still the same. For example, the words *efficiency*, *efficient*, and *efficiently* are in the same family.

Noun	Verb	Adjective	Adverb
excess	excess	excessive	excessively
maintenance	maintain	maintainable	—
expectation	expect	expectable	expectably
explanation	explain	explanatory	explanatorily
technology	—	technological	technologically

Read the Build Your Vocabulary note. Study the word family chart. Complete the sentences with the correct form of words from the chart.

1. Even experts cannot _____ why people would sacrifice their leisure time for work.

2. Mario Romano's wife says that he is on his phone _____ while the family is at the pool.

3. Most workers want a better balance between work and life, but it's not usually a _____ lifestyle.

4. Thanks to _____ improvements, people can now work from anywhere around the world.

5. Nowadays some bosses have the _____ that their employees will check in even when they are on vacation.

WHAT DO YOU THINK?

PAIRS How do you feel about technology? Do you think it has caused a work/life imbalance? Why or why not?

ON THE WEB

For more information about this topic, go online and search "work on vacation." Report back to the class.

LISTENING AND SPEAKING

Talk about wishes and dreams

GET READY TO WATCH

Miranda is talking about what she would do with a lot of money. What would you do if you had a lot more money?

WATCH

■◀ **Watch the video. Answer the questions.**

1. Where is Miranda's dream house?
2. Where is Sam's dream house?
3. Why doesn't Miranda like the mountains?
4. Why doesn't Sam like the beach?
5. What is Miranda's dream vacation?
6. What is Sam's dream vacation?

CONVERSATION

A ■◀ **Watch part of the video. Complete the conversation.**

Miranda: Wouldn't you love to live in a place like this?

Sam: Mmm. It's nice. But if I had the money to buy a dream home, I would

get a _____ in the mountains, right next to a lake.

Miranda: No, no, no, no. The beach is far _____. The mountains have too many bugs, they're too cold in the winter, and they're too lonely.

Sam: Yeah, well, the beach has too much sun and too much sand. I hate sand. And I don't like to lie around in the sun.

Miranda: If I had this house, I would lounge on my deck all day, feeling the warm

ocean _____ on my skin.

Sam: You want to live at the beach and you don't even want to go swimming?

Miranda: Oh, yes. Occasionally I would _____.

Sam: Well, in my mountain home, I would take my boat out every morning and catch fish for lunch.

B PAIRS **Practice the conversation.**

C PAIRS **Practice the conversation again. Make similar conversations. Talk about your dream home. Where would you like to live? What would you do there?**

Pronunciation Note

In sentences starting with *if*, the voice often goes down and then up a little at the end of the *if* clause. The voice goes down at the end of the sentence.

◀))) **Listen and repeat.**

If I had the money to buy a dream home,

I would get a cabin in the mountains.

If I had this house, I would

lounge on my deck all day.

WHAT DO YOU THINK?

PAIRS Miranda and Sam are dreaming of things they would do with a lot of money. Do you think having a lot of money makes people happier? Why or why not?

STUDY Present Unreal Conditional

If Clause	Result Clause
If Sam **had** a lot of money,	he **would buy** a cabin in the mountains.
If Miranda **lived** at the beach,	she **would go** swimming every day.
If Sam **were** wealthy,	he **might buy** a boat.
If Miranda **didn't have to work**,	she **would lie** on her deck all day.

Grammar Note

- Use *were* for all subjects in the *if* clause when the verb is a form of *be*.
- Don't use *would* or *might* in the *if* clause.

PRACTICE

A **Circle the correct verb forms.**

1. If Miranda (had)/ would have a lot of money, she bought /(would buy) a beach house.

2. If she **didn't have to** / **wouldn't have to** work, she **took** / **would take** a long vacation.

3. Sam **went** /**would go** fishing every day if he **had** / **would have** a boat.

4. If he **caught** / **would catch** a fish, he **ate** / **would eat** it for lunch.

5. Even if he **had** / **would have** a lot of money, Sam **traveled** / **wouldn't travel** around the world.

6. If Sam **lived** / **would live** in the mountains, he **felt** / **would feel** very relaxed.

B **On a separate piece of paper, use each pair of true statements to write a present unreal conditional sentence. Use *would* in the result clause.**

1. I have homework. I can't go to the movies tonight.

> If I didn't have homework, I would go to the movies tonight.

2. I don't have a lot of money. I can't buy a home by the beach.

3. He has to work tonight. He can't go to the movies.

4. She doesn't have a work permit. She can't get a job here.

5. I'm not a bird. I can't fly.

6. He doesn't speak the language. He doesn't feel comfortable.

7. I have to take the test. I'm nervous.

WHAT ABOUT YOU?

PAIRS Individually, complete the *if* clause in these questions on a separate piece of paper. Then, in pairs, take turns asking and answering each other's questions.

Where would you go if . . . ?   How would you feel if . . . ?

What would you do tomorrow if . . . ?   What would you say if . . . ?

Who would you call if . . . ?

GET READY

Sam is interested in majoring in education. He reads an article about an opinion on standardized testing. What standardized tests have you taken?

 STUDY THE MODEL

A Read the article. How does the author feel about the issue?

Are Standardized Tests Good for Students?

Students have to take standardized tests throughout their academic careers. Standardized tests are not a new concept. They have been part of the education system for over 150 years. However, standardized tests are hurting, rather than helping, students.

Some people think that standardized tests are objective. For example, they are often multiple-choice tests in which each question has one right answer. In my opinion, multiple-choice tests are not a good way to assess students. Real life is not that simple. Students need to be able to think critically about situations and realize there isn't always a "right" or "wrong" answer.

It can be argued that standardized tests are fair because the questions are the same for all students. But I believe standardized tests are not fair. Students from different backgrounds or with different native languages and skills all have to take the same tests. They don't have the same knowledge or ability as someone who grew up in the country. For instance, a student whose native language is English is likely to do better on a standardized test.

It is true that standardized testing may seem less expensive. However, standardized tests actually cost more money. The cost of testing students, correcting grading mistakes, and checking for accuracy hurts a state's education budget. I think that money could be better spent on teachers, books, and tests that will help a student succeed after graduation.

In conclusion, standardized tests have existed for a long time; however, they are not the best use of resources and are not the best measure of students' progress.

Writing Tip

Writers use certain **language to persuade** readers to agree with their opinion.

Emphasize Opinion	Provide Examples
I believe . . .	For example, . . .
In my opinion, . . .	For instance, . . .
Discuss Opposing Arguments	**Summarize Opinion**
It can be argued that . . .	In conclusion, . . .
Some people think that . . .	In summary, . . .
It is true that . . .	To sum up, . . .

B Read the Writing Tip on page 138. Read the article again. Underline the language of persuasion.

C Look at and complete the chart the writer used to plan his/her statement of opinion.

Topic: Standardized tests
Opinion: Standardized tests are not good for students.
Your Arguments: 1. Standardized tests are often _____ tests. Students can't think critically. 2. Standardized tests are not _____. Students whose native language is _____ usually do better on a standardized test. 3. Standardized tests actually cost _____. They hurt a state's education budget.
Opposing Arguments: 1. Standardized tests are _____. 2. Standardized tests are _____. 3. Standardized tests are _____.
Conclusion: Standardized tests are not the best use of _____ and are not the best measure of students' _____.

BEFORE YOU WRITE

You're going to write a statement of opinion about a topic you feel strongly about.
Create a chart to list your arguments and the opposing arguments.

Topic:
Your Opinion:
Your Arguments: 1. 2. 3.
Opposing Arguments: 1. 2. 3.
Conclusion:

WRITE

Review the Model and the Writing Tip. Use the ideas from your chart to write a statement of opinion.

7

Read a course schedule

GET READY

Sam has decided to get a college degree. He's looking at a course schedule online for general education classes. Have you ever looked for information about an educational program online?

PRACTICAL READING

Look at the course schedule. Read the statements. Circle *True* or *False*. Correct the false statements.

| Home | Campus News | Credit | Programs | More Courses | Map | | Search | 🔍 |

General Information for all Courses:

On-Campus courses – Preregistration for all courses is done online at the University website until the first day of classes. After the first day of classes, or if the class is full, registration can only be done by an "add" slip received from the instructor.

Fees – All fees must be paid prior to the start of the semester. (See the current calendar for deadlines and late fees.)

Assessment Tests – All entering students must first take the English and Math Assessment Tests prior to registration in any English or math class. Call or visit the University Assessment Center for a test schedule and appointment.

English 100 – Introduction to English Fundamentals
Credits: 3
Prerequisite – Placement by the English Assessment Test
English 100 is a review of English grammar, spelling, and paragraph writing. English 100 introduces reading comprehension techniques for college students, including vocabulary development.

English 101 – English Fundamentals   **Credits: 3**
Prerequisite – Introduction to English Fundamentals with a grade of C or better, or placement by the English Assessment Test.
English 101 builds on the grammar, vocabulary, reading and writing skills developed in English 100 with an emphasis on essay writing.

English 102 – College Reading and Comprehension
Credits: 5
Prerequisite – English 101 with a grade of C or better, or placement by the English Assessment Test.
English 102 teaches reading comprehension skills for the typical college-level course textbook or supplemental material, and continues with intermediate-level grammar, vocabulary, and writing skills development. English 102 emphasizes writing a multiple-page report or a paper with a bibliography.

Math 100 – Introduction to Arithmetic Fundamentals
Credits: 3
Prerequisite – Placement by the Math Assessment Test
Math 100 reviews basic arithmetic: addition, subtraction, multiplication, division, fractions, decimals, and whole numbers.

Math 101 – Introduction to Algebra   **Credits: 3**
Prerequisite – Math 100 with a grade of C or better, or placement by the Math Assessment Test
Math 101 continues the review of basic arithmetic and introduces beginning concepts of algebra.

Math 102 – Algebra   **Credits: 3**
Prerequisite – Math 101 with a grade of C or better, or placement by the Math Assessment Test
Math 102 covers algebraic concepts including rational numbers, equations, and word problems.

---

1. Before the start of classes, students have to register for courses in person.   True   False

2. If a class is full, students can still register for the course online.   True   False

3. All fees have to be paid before the semester starts.   True   False

4. First-time students can register for an English or math class without taking any tests.   True   False

5.	English 102 is a review of English grammar, spelling, and paragraph writing.		True	False
6.	Students in English 102 will read high-school-level textbooks and write a one-page report.		True	False
7.	To register for Math 101, students must pass Math 100 with a grade of C or better, or be placed in the class because of the results of their Math Assessment Test.		True	False

PRACTICAL SPEAKING

 A ◀))) **A student is talking to a clerk at the Registrar's Office about prerequisites for some of the courses. Listen and read the conversation.**

Student: Hi. I have a question about prerequisites.

Clerk: What course are you interested in?

Student: I want to take algebra.

Clerk: That's Math 102. You need to have passed Math 101. Or, after taking the Math Assessment Test, you've been placed in Math 102.

Student: So even though I haven't taken Math 101, I can still take algebra if I do well enough in the Math Assessment Test?

Clerk: Yes, that's right.

B PAIRS **Practice the conversation.**

C PAIRS **Look at the course schedule again. Role play a similar conversation between the student and the clerk about prerequisites.**

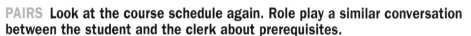

PRACTICAL LISTENING

 ◀))) **Listen to the news program about college scholarship fraud. Complete the sentences with the words from the box.**

> guarantee   eligible   fraudulent   denied   online   fee

1. College scholarship fraud happens all year round now because _____ colleges have become more popular.

2. One indication that a company is _____ is that the company promises that you will get a scholarship.

3. In fact, no company can _____ that an applicant will get a scholarship.

4. The Federal Trade Commission is reminding students to never pay a _____ in advance for a scholarship.

5. Some companies won't give your money back even if you can prove that you have been _____ for every scholarship.

6. Some companies ask you for your bank information in order to confirm that you are _____ for a scholarship.

WHAT DO YOU THINK?

PAIRS How can having a college degree be beneficial? With your partner, make a list of reasons why people get college degrees. Share your list with the class.

GET READY TO WATCH

Sam is asking his boss, Ramon, for a favor. Have you ever had to ask a boss or a teacher for a favor? What happened?

WATCH

🎥◀ **Watch the video. Circle the correct answers.**

1. Sam asks Ramon for _____.
   a. a raise
   b. time off to take classes
   c. a regular schedule

2. First, Sam needs to take _____.
   a. two classes a semester
   b. general education classes
   c. education classes

3. In a few years, Sam wants to transfer _____.
   a. to city college
   b. to the university
   c. to a psychology major

> ### Pronunciation Note
>
> English words can begin with one, two, or even three consonant sounds. They can end with up to four consonant sounds. We say the consonants closely together.
>
> ◀)) **Listen and repeat.**
>
> transfer   a fixed schedule
>
> placement tests
>
> You're smart to start off slow.
>
> I think it's great that you've got a plan.

CONVERSATION

A 🎥◀ **Watch part of the video. Complete the conversation.**

Ramon: So what's the plan? What do you want to study?

Sam: Well, first I need to do general _____ classes. I can do those at City College. Then I hope to transfer here to get my BA.

Ramon: That's great, Sam. Good for you! How many classes are you going to take?

Sam: I'm just going to start with one. It's been _____ since I was in school, you know.

Ramon: How long will it take you to finish?

Sam: Oh, it'll be a few years before I can transfer.

B PAIRS **Practice the conversation. Use your own names.**

C PAIRS **Practice the conversation again. Make similar conversations. Talk about your long-term goal and the steps you will take to reach that goal.**

WHAT DO YOU THINK?

PAIRS What if Ramon says he can't give Sam a fixed schedule? What should Sam do? Should he pursue his goal anyway? What would you do if you were Sam?

@RafikAramayan *Today*
Now that the interview is over, it's time for a follow-up letter!

GET READY

After his interview at CloseFit, Rafik sends the interviewer a follow-up email.
What is the purpose of a follow-up message?

WRITE A FOLLOW-UP MESSAGE AFTER A JOB INTERVIEW

**Read Rafik's follow-up message and match the purposes (1–5) to the parts.
Write the correct numbers in the blanks.**

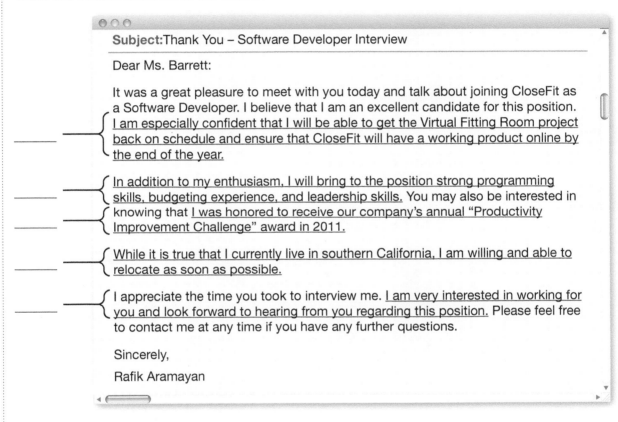

Subject: Thank You – Software Developer Interview

Dear Ms. Barrett:

It was a great pleasure to meet with you today and talk about joining CloseFit as a Software Developer. I believe that I am an excellent candidate for this position. I am especially confident that I will be able to get the Virtual Fitting Room project back on schedule and ensure that CloseFit will have a working product online by the end of the year.

In addition to my enthusiasm, I will bring to the position strong programming skills, budgeting experience, and leadership skills. You may also be interested in knowing that I was honored to receive our company's annual "Productivity Improvement Challenge" award in 2011.

While it is true that I currently live in southern California, I am willing and able to relocate as soon as possible.

I appreciate the time you took to interview me. I am very interested in working for you and look forward to hearing from you regarding this position. Please feel free to contact me at any time if you have any further questions.

Sincerely,

Rafik Aramayan

1. Repeats things you said during the interview about your specific skills and qualifications.
2. Responds to any specific challenges the company is facing mentioned by the interviewer.
3. Says something in the message you forgot to say during the interview.
4. Expresses strong interest in working for the company.
5. Responds to any objections the interviewer brought.

PUT YOUR IDEAS TO WORK

@RafikAramayan *Today*
I just got a call from CloseFit. They offered me a job!

A Imagine that you went to a job interview and thought that it went very well. Using Rafik's message as a model, write a follow-up email message to the interviewer.

B PAIRS A follow-up message can also be sent by mail. What are the advantages and disadvantages of using email compared to regular mail? If you were Rafik, would you send your follow-up message by email or mail? Why?

GRAMMAR

In this unit, you studied:
* Embedded questions
* Present unreal conditional

See page 154 for your Grammar Review.

VOCABULARY See page 161 for the Unit 10 Vocabulary.

Vocabulary Learning Strategy: Learn words that go together

A Find words from the list that are used together. Fill in the missing words.

placement _____   prior _____   _____ posted

_____ education   _____ a dip   stick _____

_____ going   work _____   sort _____

**B Circle 5 groups of words that are used together in Exercise A.
Write a sentence with each word.**

SPELLING See page 161 for the Unit 10 Vocabulary.

CLASS **Choose 10 words for a spelling test.**

LISTENING PLUS

A Watch each video. Write the story of Sam's day on a separate piece of paper.

> *Sam is at the Career Counseling Center speaking to Tonya. He wants to explore
> some career opportunities. Tonya asks Sam some questions to help him find out
> what he'd like to do.*

B PAIRS Review the conversation in Lesson 4. (See page 136.)
Role play the conversation for the class.

NOW I CAN

PAIRS See page 131 for the Unit 10 Goals. **Check ✓ the things you can do.
Underline the things you want to study more. Tell your partner.**

> I can _____. I need more practice with _____.

COORDINATION WITH *SO, TOO, EITHER,* AND *NEITHER*

Read Diana's and Lena's descriptions of themselves. On a separate piece of paper, write two sentences about what the two women have in common, using *so*, *too*, *either*, and *neither*.

My name is Diana Nhan. I work at Sundale University in the Business Department office. I'm 38 years old and married. I like to garden and to cook. My husband and I don't go out a lot, but we have a dinner party about once a month. Sometimes we go to the movies. We don't get much exercise, so we try to take a walk every evening.

My name is Lena Panich. I work at Sundale University in the IT Department. I'm 32 years old and married. I don't have children. I like to cook, so we don't go out to restaurants very often. We like to go to the movies, though. We are thinking about joining a gym because we don't get enough exercise.

1. (work)

> Diana works at Sundale University, and so does Lena.
> Diana works at Sundale University, and Lena does, too.

2. (married)
3. (cook)
4. (go out)
5. (go to the movies)
6. (get exercise)

SIMPLE PAST AND PRESENT PERFECT

Complete the conversation between Diana and Paula. Use the simple past and the present perfect.

Diana: _____Did_____ anyone _____call_____ while I was out?
1. call

Paula: Emily from Campus Facilities _____ at 11:30.
2. call

Diana: What _____ she _____?
3. say

Paula: She _____ the security request for the conference yet.
4. not receive

Diana: That's strange. I _____ it in the campus mail yesterday.
5. put

Paula: No one _____ up the mail since yesterday morning.
6. pick

Diana: You're kidding! What's going on?

Paula: I don't know. I _____ three phone calls so far, but no one is answering in the mailroom.
7. make

Diana: That's strange.

PRESENT PERFECT AND PRESENT PERFECT CONTINUOUS

Read part of Ahmed's résumé. Complete the sentences about Ahmed, using the present perfect or the present perfect continuous. Use the present perfect continuous if the action is continuing.

Work Experience

Car salesman, Bronson Trucks	2011 – present
Salesclerk, Big Buy Electronics	2008 – 2011

Education

Middletown Business College	2013 – present (6 units completed)
Longtown City College	2006 – 2008

1. Ahmed _____*has had*_____ (have) two jobs.

2. He _____ (work) in sales-related jobs since 2008.

3. He _____ (sell) cars since 2011.

4. He _____ (take) classes at Midtown Business College since 2013.

5. He _____ (complete) six units.

6. He _____ (not earn) earned a degree.

7. He _____ (study) at two different colleges.

WOULD RATHER AND *WOULD PREFER*

**Ben and Ahmed are discussing the kind of work they would like.
Complete the conversation with *rather*, *prefer*, *to*, and *than*.**

Ahmed: Would you _____*rather*_____ work at a large company or a small company?
1.

Ben: I'd prefer a large company _____ a small one.
2.

Ahmed: Why?

Ben: Because there are more opportunities for promotion, of course. Would you _____ to work
3.
at a small company?

Ahmed: Yeah, I think I would. In a small company, you learn about all parts of the business, not just your
own job. I'd _____ not be so specialized.
4.

Ben: I guess. But large companies have offices all over the world. I'd _____ travel and work in
5.
other countries _____ stay in one town.
6.

Ahmed: Not me. I'd _____ to stay here with my family.
7.

Ben: Well, I'd _____ a large salary. Then I could visit my family whenever I wanted.
8.

Ahmed: Yeah, I think everyone would _____ make a large salary _____ a small one!
9.   10.

GRAMMAR REVIEW

PAST PERFECT

Event *a* happened before event *b*. Complete the sentences using the simple past and the past perfect.

1. a. The pedestrian started crossing the street.
   b. The van pulled into the intersection.

   When the van _pulled into the intersection_, the pedestrian _had started crossing the street_.

2. a. The light turned green.
   b. The pedestrian stepped into the crosswalk.

   The light _____ when the pedestrian _____.

3. a. The pedestrian walked halfway across the intersection.
   b. The van turned in front of the pedestrian.

   When the van _____, the pedestrian _____.

4. a. A police officer saw the whole thing.
   b. The van drove away.

   The van _____, but the police officer _____.

5. a. The driver didn't notice the pedestrian.
   b. The driver felt bad.

   The driver _____ because he _____.

6. a. The driver apologized to the police officer.
   b. The police officer gave him a ticket.

   The driver _____, but the police officer

   _____ anyway.

GERUNDS AS SUBJECTS AND OBJECTS

Complete the conversation with the gerund form of the verbs from the box.

(improve ~~train~~ postpone find fire work tell)

Emily: How are things working out with your new helper?

Lena: Oh, _training_ people is so difficult. He's having some problems.
         ‾‾‾‾1.

Emily: That's too bad. Is Tom thinking about _____ him?
                                                    ‾‾2.

Lena: No, things haven't gotten that bad yet. _____ a new person would be an even bigger
                                                   ‾‾3.
         problem. And in some ways, he's very good at the job.

Emily: Well, is he interested in _____?
                                     ‾‾4.

Lena: I think so, but it would be much easier if I just had to explain something technical. _____
                                                                                                ‾‾5.
         someone how to behave is much harder.

Emily: But the sooner you talk to him, the better. _____ these kinds of things is never a good idea.
                                                        ‾‾6.

Lena: You're right. I plan on _____ closely with him starting tomorrow.
                                  ‾‾7.

TAG QUESTIONS

Complete the sentences with tag questions.

1. The training is at 4:00, _____isn't it_____?
2. They'll escort employees to the meeting, _____?
3. I need to report any incidents to the manager, _____?
4. The orientation isn't over yet, _____?
5. The new employees were here yesterday, _____?
6. She has already gotten a permit, _____?
7. He hadn't seen the presentation before, _____?
8. He referred to the employee handbook, _____?

IT + *BE* + ADJECTIVE + INFINITIVE

Read the welcome email. Complete the sentences with ideas from the email. Use *it* + *be* + adjectives in parentheses + infinitive.

Subject: Welcome New Employees!

❶I'm so happy to welcome you to our campus. ❷Learning the routines of a new job can be challenging. ❸And getting familiar with such a large campus is a little difficult! ❹Please ask anyone on the security team for help when you need it. ❺I think that you'll enjoy working with college students. ❻Taking time to know them is important. ❼Learning about their stories is interesting, and it can also make you a better security officer. ❽Of course, dealing with the few problem students is not so easy. But the entire department is here to support you. ❾Talking to a coworker at the first sign of trouble is a great idea. And my door is always open.

Welcome aboard!

Ramon Sanchez

---

1. ____It's great to welcome____ (great) you to our campus.
2. _____ can _____ (challenging) the routines of a new job.
3. _____ (not easy) familiar with such a large campus.
4. _____ (fine) anyone on the security team for help.
5. _____ (fun) with college students.
6. _____ (important) to know the students.
7. _____ (enjoyable) about students' stories.
8. _____ (difficult) the few problem students.
9. _____ (helpful) to a coworker at the first sign of trouble.

MODALS FOR ADVICE

**Complete the conversation between Emily and her teenage son.
Circle the correct modals of advice.**

Emily: Where are you going? You (1) should / had better not eat breakfast before you go to school!

Jesse: I'm not hungry. I (2) shouldn't / ought to eat when I'm not hungry.

Emily: Yes, you (3) should / had better not. You (4) ought / should to have a little something at least. How about a piece of toast?

Jesse: OK. (5) Shouldn't / Ought we have wheat bread instead of white bread? You want to be healthy, right?

Emily: Yes, you're right. I (6) should / ought buy some next time I go to the store. Where is your brother?

Jesse: He's probably still sleeping. (7) Ought / Should I wake him up?

Emily: Sleeping!? He (8) shouldn't / had better get up right away! He's going to be late!

FUTURE CONTINUOUS

Look at the agenda. Write sentences using the future continuous.

CONFERENCE AGENDA

8:30 – 9:00	Breakfast
9:00 – 10:00	Opening speaker
10:00 – 12:00	Lectures
12:00 – 1:00	Lunch
1:00 – 4:00	Group meetings
4:00 – 5:00	Plan for next year

1. (eat) *From 8:30 to 9:00, they will be eating breakfast.*

2. (listen to) _____

3. (attend) _____

4. (have) _____

5. (participate in) _____

6. (plan) _____

THE PASSIVE VOICE

Complete the letter of complaint, using the passive voice.

○○○

Subject: Billing Error

Dear Mr. Andrews:

I am writing this email to follow up on the conversation I had with

Customer Service Agent Julie Patel, regarding my Oct. 1 cell phone bill.

I _was charged_ for using too many minutes, but I did not make or receive
    1. charge

the phone calls on the bill. On Oct. 3, I _____ not to worry about
                        2. tell

the charges. The agent said that TelCo would remove them. But the charges

_____. I _____ a new bill on Nov. 1st. It said the
  3. not deduct   **4. send**

charges were now overdue. I called again and _____ a new bill
                         5. promise

without the extra charges. At that time, I _____ your name and
                        6. give

email address and told to follow up with you.

Thank you for your attention to this matter.

Diana Wu

ADJECTIVE CLAUSES

Read the paragraph. Underline the relative pronouns. Cross out the relative pronouns that can be omitted.

    Diana enjoys working at the business conference because she always meets interesting people there. Last year she met a woman who started selling cookies out of her house and ended up as the president of a large cookie company. One man that she met was the CEO of a large corporation before he became a college professor. He had a lot of knowledge that he was happy to share with everyone. Diana has met people who come from the other side of the country to attend the conference. They come because the information that they get at the conference is very valuable. Also, it's good to meet and share ideas with other people who work in your field. Diana isn't a businessperson, but she likes the people who she meets at the conference.

PLACEMENT OF DIRECT AND INDIRECT OBJECTS

Write six sentences about each picture, using the verb provided. Use a direct object and an indirect object in each sentence.

give

1. *He's giving her flowers.*
2. *He's giving flowers to her.*
3. *He's giving them to her.*
4. _____
5. _____
6. _____

show

1. _____
2. _____
3. _____
4. _____
5. _____
6. _____

MODALS OF POSSIBILITY AND CONCLUSION

Complete the paragraphs with the words from the box.

| can't be | could | may not | might be | must not | ~~must be~~ |

Rochelle is speaking loudly and waving her hands in the air. She ___*must be*___
                                                                              1.

excited. Ben keeps looking at his computer. He _____ bored with
                                                          2.

Rochelle's story. Or, he _____ just be busy today.
                                    3.

It's lunchtime. Karen usually brings a sandwich and eats it at her desk, but she's

eating at the cafeteria. She _____ have her sandwich today. Arnold is
                                        4.

sitting next to Karen. They're talking and laughing. Karen _____ upset
                                                                        5.

with him. Maybe Karen doesn't know about the gossip. Or, she _____
                                                                        6.

care at all.

REPORTED SPEECH: STATEMENTS AND IMPERATIVES

Read the conversation. Write each statement as reported speech. Use *said*.

Lena: Our shower doesn't work.

Landlord: The water heater is brand new!

Lena: That isn't the problem. The water doesn't come out.

Landlord: Try turning the faucet harder.

Lena: We already tried that! We can't get it to work.

Landlord: Don't worry. I'll call the plumber.

Lena: Call me back with the appointment time!

1. _Lena said (that) their shower didn't work._

2. _____

3. _____

4. _____

5. _____

6. _____

7. _____

ADVERB CLAUSES OF TIME

Read the order of events. Answer the questions with complete sentences. Use *when, after, before, as soon as,* or *until* in your answer.

1. Marcos applied for the Tech Assistant job. Later, he became Lena's assistant.
When did Marcos become Lena's assistant?
He became Lena's assistant after he applied for the Tech Assistant job.

2. Marcos learned how to repair computers. Then he applied for the university job.
When did Marcos learn how to repair computers?

3. He started working at the university. Immediately, he began to learn new things.
When did he begin to learn new things?

4. He keeps working on a computer. He stops when the job is finished.
How long does he keep working on a computer?

5. He saw Lena talking to her boss. He knew there might be a problem.
When did he know there might be a problem?

6. Lena spoke to him about his behavior with people. Then he tried to be friendlier.
When did he try to be friendlier?

PHRASAL VERBS

Complete the paragraph with the phrasal verbs from the box.

| drop off | filled out | help out | count on | picked up | found out | ~~wrote down~~ |

Emily has a very busy day at work today. In the morning, she ___*wrote down*___
1.

everything she needed to do so she wouldn't forget anything. Then she

_____ a work order for some classroom repairs. She went to Sal's
2.

office to _____ the work order for his signature. On her way back,
3.

she _____ a key from the secretary. When she got back to her
4.

office, she _____ that Gina was working. She hopes that she can
5.

_____ Gina to _____ with some of the errands she
6.   7.

needs to do.

ADVERB CLAUSES OF REASON

Read each conversation. Write two sentences based on Emily's answers, using adverb clauses of reason. More than one answer is possible for each one.

1. **Gina:** Why do you want to live in a smaller home?

   Emily: It will be easier to take care of.

   Emily wants to live in a smaller home because it will be easier to take care of.

   Since it will be easier to take care of, Emily wants to live in a smaller home.

2. **Gina:** Why do your sons have so many belongings?

   Emily: They have a lot of hobbies.

   _____

   _____

3. **Gina:** Why is living in an apartment easier?

   Emily: I don't have to do yard work or household maintenance.

   _____

   _____

4. **Gina:** Why aren't your sons upset about moving to a smaller home?

   Emily: They are leaving for college soon.

   _____

   _____

EMBEDDED QUESTIONS

Read the questions on the flyer. Rewrite them as embedded questions.

> Where can I find a job?
> What jobs are available?
> Am I qualified?
> Do I need training?
> Who is hiring?
> How do I write an effective résumé?
> **Get Answers at the Job Center!**
>
> JOB CENTER

1. *I wonder where I can find a job.*
2. I don't know _____
3. I'd like to know _____
4. Can you tell me _____
5. I'm not sure _____
6. Can you explain _____

PRESENT UNREAL CONDITIONAL

Use an idea from each side of the chart. Write sentences in the present unreal conditional. More than one answer may be possible.

1.	Sam has young children	he has a lot of friends
2.	Sam works at a university	he has such good benefits
3.	Sam doesn't have a lot of money	his boss will give him time off to study
4.	Sam doesn't have a lot of time	he can't afford to study full time
5.	Sam works with nice people	he enjoys his job
6.	Sam works hard	he's so busy in the evenings
7.	Sam is friendly	he can't take more than one class

1. *If Sam didn't have young children, he wouldn't be so busy in the evenings.*
2. _____
3. _____
4. _____
5. _____
6. _____
7. _____

GRAMMAR REFERENCES

UNIT 2, LESSON 2, PAGE 21

Non-action Verbs

Emotions	Mental States	Wants and Preferences	Appearance and Value
admire	agree	hope	appear
adore	assume	need	be
appreciate	believe	prefer	cost
care	consider	want	equal
dislike	disagree	wish	look (seem)
doubt	expect		matter
fear	guess	**The Senses**	represent
hate	hope	feel	resemble
like	imagine	hear	seem
love	know	notice	weigh
regret	mean	see	
respect	mind	smell	
trust	realize	sound	
	recognize	taste	
Possession and Relationship	remember		
belong	see (understand)		
contain	suppose		
have	think (believe)		
own	understand		
possess	wonder		

UNIT 3, LESSON 5, PAGE 39

Gerunds as Objects of Prepositions

Verb + Preposition

admit to	complain about	insist on	rely on
advise against	count on	keep on	resort to
apologize for	deal with	look forward to	succeed in
approve of	dream about/of	object to	talk about
believe in	feel like/about	pay for	think about
choose between/among	go along with	plan on	wonder about

Adjective + Preposition

afraid of	careful of	good at	satisfied with
amazed at/by	concerned about	happy about	shocked at/by
angry at	curious about	interested in	sick of
ashamed of	different from	nervous about	sorry for/about
aware of	excited about	opposed to	surprised at/about/by
awful at	famous for	ready for	terrible at
bad at	fed up with	responsible for	tired of
bored with/by	fond of	sad about	used to
capable of	glad about	safe from	worried about

GRAMMAR REFERENCES

UNIT 9, LESSON 2, PAGE 119

Phrasal Verbs: Separable

Phrasal Verb	Meaning	Phrasal Verb	Meaning
bring . . . up	raise (children)	look . . . up	try to find (in a book, etc.)
bring . . . up	call attention to	make . . . up	invent
call . . . back	return a phone call	pass . . . up	decide not to use
call . . . off	cancel	pay . . . back	repay
check . . . out	examine	pick . . . out	choose
cheer . . . up	cause to feel happier	pick . . . up	lift; stop to get
clean . . . up	clean completely	point . . . out	indicate
clear . . . up	explain	put . . . away	put in an appropriate place
close . . . down	close by force	put . . . back	return to its original place
cover . . . up	cover completely	put . . . off	delay
cross . . . out	draw a line through	put . . . together	assemble
cut . . . up	cut into small pieces	set . . . up	prepare for use
do . . . over	do again	shut . . . off	stop (a machine, etc.)
figure . . . out	understand	sign . . . up	register
fill . . . in	complete with information	start . . . over	start again
fill . . . out	complete (a form)	take . . . back	return
fill . . . up	fill completely	talk . . . into	persuade
find . . . out	learn information	talk . . . over	discuss
give . . . back	return	tear . . . down	destroy
give . . . up	quit, abandon	think . . . over	consider
hand . . . in	submit	throw . . . away	put in the trash
hand . . . out	distribute	turn . . . down	lower the volume; reject
help . . . out	assist	turn . . . off	stop (a machine, etc.)
leave . . . out	omit	turn . . . on	start (a machine, etc.)
let . . . down	disappoint	turn . . . up	make louder
look . . . over	examine	write . . . down	write on a piece of paper

Phrasal Verbs: Inseparable

Phrasal Verb	Meaning	Phrasal Verb	Meaning
count on	depend on	get over	feel better after something bad
fall for	feel romantic love for	look after	take care of
get off	leave (a bus, train, etc.)	look into	investigate
get on	board (a bus, train, etc.)	run into	meet accidentally
get through	finish	stick with	not quit, not leave

WORD LIST

UNIT 1

Lesson 1
awful
a dean
follow
no wonder
packed
a reception
a romantic comedy
the staff

Lesson 4
a conference
distracted

a file folder
furious
misplace
ordinary
a participant
a stack

Lesson 6
affect
ban
despite
diabetes
eventual

fiction
medical
obesity
a policy
a restriction

Lesson 8
catch up
cross off
overwhelmed
panic
pile up
prioritize

satisfying
a supply

Job-Seeking Skills
absolutely
benefits
a bonus
necessary
preferred

UNIT 2

Lesson 1
an acceptance
a BA
a degree
an MBA
a promotion
a reduction
the registrar
a responsibility
the tuition

Lesson 3
a challenge
a committee
creative
an expert
innovative
a strategy

a task
volunteer

Lesson 4
additional
attach
a budget
a coordinator
a cut
encourage
initiative
request
update

Lesson 7
deductions
FICA (Federal Insurance
   Contributions Act)
gross pay

HI (Hospital Insurance)
net pay
OASDI (Old Age,
   Survivors, and
   Disability Insurance)
overtime pay
regular pay
withholdings
YTD (year-to-date)

Lesson 8
bother
a demonstration
a display
a feature
a flash drive
insert
a jam

makeup
reset
training

Job-Seeking Skills
communication
construction
a database
leadership
maintenance
specific
transferable

UNIT 3

Lesson 1
cooperative
damaged
fault
a sedan
shaken up
a siren
smash
stick around
totaled
a witness

Lesson 4
anxious
an attitude
complicated
install
a priority
rearrange
upgrade

Lesson 6
apologize
a claim
a contact

documentation
factual
file
legally
prevent
a punishment

Lesson 8
an adjustment
a big deal
crucial
demanding
plenty

preliminary
run
smoothly

Job-Seeking Skills
competitive
the content
dedicated
desired
a facility
mobile
motivated
versatile

UNIT 4

Lesson 1
allowed
escort
an incident
a meter
an orientation
a permit
refer
remind
a violation

Lesson 3
an alert
available
despair

frustrated
indicate
recklessly
a resident
a sensor

Lesson 4
bankrupt
deserve
end up
get by
immediate family
a point
relieved

retirement
sick leave

Lesson 6
alertness
an authorization
drowsiness
habit-forming
a prescription
prohibit
a refill
side effects
a tablet
transfer

Lesson 8
the faculty
a fee
a midterm
outrageous
a petition
a shortage
valid

Job-Seeking Skills
a connection
freelance
a profile
a recommendation
a seeker

WORD LIST

UNIT 5

Lesson 1
a carb
cut down on
perks
tempting
tend
a track
a treadmill
willpower
work study

Lesson 3
an advance
cholesterol
circulation

entertain
leisure
occasionally
passively
sedentary

Lesson 4
arrange
a caterer
a continental breakfast
definite
a fountain
a plaza
run
supervise

Lesson 7
an allergy
arthritis
asthma
hepatitis
hospitalize
irregular
pregnant
thyroid
tuberculosis
a tumor

Lesson 8
appreciate
eavesdrop
forgetful

a genius
overhear
personality
stereotype

Job-Seeking Skills
analyze
bilingual
a client
effective
an objective
proficient
a qualification
a reference
a solution

UNIT 6

Lesson 1
deduct
discontinue
extend
permission
premier
a release
a subscription
a trial

Lesson 3
detach
due
a due date

the make
nonoperation
a penalty
renew
the VIN

Lesson 4
can't place
economics
heavyset
a lobby
the specifics
step in
transfer

Lesson 6
approve
a coupon
deliberately
estimate
noticeable
tricky
trust

Lesson 8
apparently
a nuisance
slam
sneak

trapped
wildlife

Job-Seeking Skills
a candidate
consideration
convenience
demonstrate
a salutation
suitability

WORD LIST

UNIT 7

Lesson 1
chaos
coordinate
make
practically
a program
react
staff

Lesson 3
adore
consequently
a credit

distribute
isolated
motivation
require
research
tutor

Lesson 4
altogether
annoyed
a gossip
hilarious
indigestion

involved
a stretch
a workaholic

Lesson 7
an annual percentage
   rate
a disclosure
finance
a fraud
a grace period
a gross annual income
a maiden name

a mortgage
a transaction
variable

Lesson 8
aggressive
a balance transfer
a debt
a fortune
lure
pass up
a prospect
a waste

UNIT 8

Lesson 1
block
clogged
drain
a handyman
replace
resist
a sewer
stopped up
weird

Lesson 3
a clause
expire
habitable

a lease
maintenance
a (security) deposit
a tenant
a utility

Lesson 4
come along
consult
efficient
enthusiastic
focused
irritated
snap
spot

Lesson 6
an accessory
a confirmation
consumable
exchange
inspect
an invoice
a manual
a refund
reject
securely

Lesson 8
defective
existing

get around to
headphones
inquire
a replacement
a routine
volume

Job-Seeking Skills
a delay
dynamic
enroll
a presentation
relocate
reorganization
turn around

WORD LIST

Lesson 1
a custodian
dusty
an errand
glossy
major
a mark
minor
a packet

Lesson 3
an alteration
a burglary
hereafter
liable

the premises
remedy
sublet
termination
vandalism

Lesson 4
acquire
belongings
a charity
decent
a nightmare
settled in
stuff
tag

Lesson 6
accompanying
a bookmobile
coach
extracurricular
hesitant
individual
an issue
literacy
participate

Lesson 8
a booth
delegate
a display

eager
generous
monitor
oversee

Job-Seeking Skills
advancement
enthusiasm
momentum
outgoing
ownership
troubleshoot
unfilled
wrap up

Lesson 1
appeal
current
fulfillment
a GED
generate
an option
sort out
a survey

Lesson 3
a curse
excessive
legitimate
mentally

overflowing
a phenomenon
portable
sacrifice
stranded

Lesson 4
a breeze
a cabin
a cruise
a deck
figures (or "that figures")
lounge
superior
take a dip

Lesson 7
algebra
arithmetic
an assessment
a deadline
eligible
fraudulent
fundamentals
guarantee
a prerequisite
prior to
supplemental

Lesson 8
accommodate
ages

fixed
general education
get going
keep posted
a placement test
stick with
work around

Job-Seeking Skills
ensure
objection
productivity
regarding

CREDITS